VIEW OF COPPS HILL, BOSTON.

EPITAPHS

FROM

COPP'S HILL BURIAL GROUND BOSTON

WITH NOTES

"TAKE THEM, O DEATH! AND BEAR AWAY
WHATEVER THOU CANST CALL THINE OWN;
THINE IMAGE, STAMPED UPON THIS CLAY,
DOES GIVE THEE THAT, BUT THAT ALONE.

TAKE THEM, O GRAVE! AND LET THEM LIE,
FOLDED UPON THY NARROW SHELVES,
AS GARMENTS BY THE SOLE LAID BY,
AND PRECIOUS ONLY TO OURSELVES.

TAKE THEM, O GREAT ETERNITY!
OUR LITTLE LIFE IS BUT A GUST
THAT BENDS THE BRANCHES OF THY TREE,
AND TRAILS ITS BLOSSOMS IN THE DUST."
                    —LONGFELLOW.

Thomas Bridgman

HERITAGE BOOKS
2024

HERITAGE BOOKS

AN IMPRINT OF HERITAGE BOOKS, INC.

Books, CDs, and more—Worldwide

For our listing of thousands of titles see our website
at
www.HeritageBooks.com

A Facsimile Reprint
Published 2024 by
HERITAGE BOOKS, INC.
Publishing Division
5810 Ruatan Street
Berwyn Heights, MD 20740

Boston and Cambridge:
James Munroe and Company.
1851

— Publisher's Notice —
In reprints such as this, it is often not possible to remove
blemishes from the original. We feel the contents of this
book warrant its reissue despite these blemishes and
hope you will agree and read it with pleasure.

International Standard Book Number
Paperbound: 978-1-55613-205-6

Copp's Hill Cemetery.

Come, let us turn
Through yon untrodden avenue, and muse
Where rest the ancient dead. Lo, what a throng
Have given their fleshly vestments to the worm,
'Neath these still shades! Here, first the forest sons
Buried their smitten people, ere the feet
Of our pale race invaded them — to die.
— Thou, who dost pore amid yon mouldering stones
So patiently, deciphering the trace
That the dull tooth of Time hath worn away,
Canst tell me where the Pilgrim fathers sleep,
Who with their ploughshare stirred this rocky glebe,
And taught the echoes of the wilderness
The voice of psalm and prayer?

Methinks even now,
From their unnoted sepulchres they warn
Alike the idler and the man of care
How soon to Death's forgotten cell shall speed
The shuttle of their days. For all her sons,
With saddest sigh of hollow-breathing winds,

Soft, vernal tears, and winter's naked boughs,
Our mother Nature mourns.
                    She tells how vain
The pride that lurks in gorgeous monuments.
The pyramid, the stained sarcophagus,
Betray their trust.   Still, there's a life that lives
Amid the mouldering clay, and silent clings
To human sympathies.   We speak to them
Who speak no more, — and listen for their words,
Forgetful that the interminable veil
Is drawn between us.
                Yet they have a voice,
A tombstone witness to the holy truths
That cannot die; and may our pulseless hearts
Wear worthily the dear Redeemer's sign, —
"Yea, saith the Spirit, — blessed are the dead
That die in Him."
                          L. H. S.

TO THE

HON. JOHN PRESCOTT BIGELOW,

MAYOR OF BOSTON,

AND TO

THE CITIZENS OF BOSTON,

This Volume

IS RESPECTFULLY DEDICATED BY THEIR HUMBLE SERVANT,

THE COMPILER.

Introduction.

THERE are few passages in the Scriptures more touching than the simple and unadorned narrative of the visit of our Lord Jesus Christ to the afflicted family in Bethany, when he met Martha, while her sister Mary " rose up hastily and went out " to the grave of Lazarus, to weep there. It teaches us to hallow the spot where our departed friends repose.

The Hebrew has ever been noted for regarding with veneration the sepulchres of his ancestors — a trait of character connected with love of country, filial affection, and all the endearments of domestic life. To this day, the devout sons of Abraham, wherever in the wide world they may dwell, look forward to a pilgrimage to Palestine, as the great and most sacred act of their lives ; and often the aged Jew seeks to lay his bones in Judea, where his fathers sleep. Although a dark cloud now rests on that doomed land, yet numerous are the monuments and sepulchres which environ the holy city ; and the " tombs of the kings " and the burial-caves of the patriarchs attract the notice of every traveller, and awaken his sympathy.

The Greeks were no less remarkable for paying honors to the dead. Their obsequies did not cease at the burial. They cherished the memory of their friends with monuments and inscriptions, and sanctified the place of interment with a veneration which might raise a blush in some Christian mourners in our own land. The *Via Sacra*, from Athens to Eleusis, passed by Ceramicus, their public cemetery, where the ruins of many splendid sepulchres are still extant.

Nor were the Romans less distinguished for this sacred and refined respect for the ashes of their ancestors. They buried their dead near the great highways, so that their memory might be ever before them; from whence comes SISTE, VIATOR— Pause, traveller, at this spot. Lofty sepulchres and marble monuments still survive among the ruins of the Eternal City, on the Appian Way. Whose heart does not burn within him, when he reads in Cicero — when he was quæstor in Sicily — of his discovery of the tomb of Archimedes among thorns and briers, with the cylinder and sphere upon it, which Marcellus had raised to his memory nearly two centuries before?

The preservation of the memory of our ancestors by tombstones and monuments in hallowed spots is honorable to our nature, and conducive to the cultivation of better and holier feelings. We are too apt to forget the lives and characters of those who adorned the circle of another generation; and, amidst the cares of life, and the absorbing pursuits of the hour, friends and connections once dear to society, when they have left us, are too often buried in the grave of oblivion. Every step, therefore, which tends to bring them up to memory, and recall their actions when alive, though it may appear a humble labor in itself, is valuable in its influence.

"It is wise for us to recur to the history of our ancestors. Those who are regardless of their ancestors and of their posterity — who do not look upon themselves as a link connecting the past with the future, in the transmissions of life from their ancestors to their posterity — do not perform their duty to the world. To be faithful to ourselves, we must keep our ancestors and posterity within reach and grasp of our thoughts and affections — living in the memory and retrospection of the past, and hoping with affection and care for those who are to come after us. We are true to ourselves only when we act with becoming pride for the blood we inherit, and which we are to transmit to those who shall soon fill our places." — DANIEL WEBSTER's Speech, Dec. 22, 1845.

With feelings, therefore, which are canonized by the good

and great of all countries, and of every age, we may approach
the subject matter of this volume of epitaphs, gathered by a
humble gleaner in the fields of the dead — the dead who lie in
one of the ancient churchyards of the PILGRIMS OF NEW
ENGLAND. The favorable reception of the "Inscriptions on
the Gravestones in Northampton" is a harbinger that such
labor will not be in vain.

The venerable cemetery on Copp's Hill is worthy of the
researches of the antiquary; for there many of the fathers
of New England were buried. With perseverance and much
pains-taking, he has pursued his object, and has collected a
large number of epitaphs and inscriptions, some of which are
connected with historical events, and others with the early prosperity of this city. Many families, too, are personally interested in this garden of the dead; for there their progenitors
repose, where the rains and the frosts are fast obliterating every
impression of lithography.

In this manner a record may be handed down to other times,
and a permanent transcript preserved, when the marble slab,
the heraldic monument, and the fading slate have crumbled into
dust. Surely, then, such an enterprise deserves a liberal encouragement. Like ourselves, the ancient Jews wrote their
inscriptions on slabs of marble, and placed them upright at the
graves of the deceased, when more splendid monuments were
not erected. But the stone and the marble have long since
mouldered into dust, and few sepulchres can now be identified.
There was then no TYPE in existence to give an everlasting
duration to their names. The Valley of Jehoshaphat was the
great place of burial for the inhabitants of Jerusalem. It ex-
tends from the Mount of Olives to Mount Moriah, and is full of
sepulchres. In its depths are the Brook Cedron and the Pool
of Siloam. Next to the holy sepulchre, no spot in Palestine is
more solemnized by sacred reminiscences ; yet, with the ex-
ception of the tombs of David, Absalom, and a few others,
the darkness of oblivion rests on this valley of the dead.

The sweetest remembrances and highest motives to Christian

duty are intertwined with, and strengthened by, meditating on
our departed friends, and making the home of the dead soothing
to the eye and sacred to the feelings; and more especially in
a Bible land, in which, when we go to the grave to weep there,
we weep not as those who have no hope.

Distinct from the respect and affection we owe to our friends
who have gone, there is another consideration of weight — the
benefit which a preservation of such memorials may confer.
They may enable heirs, in some instances, to prove their descent and trace their genealogy; they may excite the young to
emulate the deeds of their honored ancestors; and they teach
us, amidst the bustle and business of the hour, that the glory of
this world passeth away. They stand like road-guides in the
journey of life, casting their long shadows over the whole path
to another world.

British heraldry is often connected with British history; and
the coat of arms — though sometimes bestowed on unworthy
objects — may reflect the lustre of other times on descendants
whose virtues and talents have been veiled by misfortune, or
buried in undeserved obscurity. What armorial ensigns may
be to the living, the faithful and judicious epitaph is to the
meritorious dead.

It was by exploring the catacombs, obelisks, and monuments
erected to the dead more than forty centuries ago, that Cham-
pollion discovered a key to Egyptian history, so happily and
eloquently elucidated by George R. Gliddon, Esq., at the Lowell lectures, in this city, a few years since.

A brief account of the celebrated spot where so many of the
founders of Boston were gathered to their fathers may not be
without interest to the numerous descendants of the deceased,
and to the stranger who visits this city.

Boston was called by the Indians Shawmut, — which signi-
fies "living fountains," for this peninsula abounded in springs,
— and by the English at Charlestown, Tri-mountain, either from
three lofty hills, visible afar off, Beacon, Copp's, and Fort Hills,
or from Beacon mountain alone, on which were "three little

rising hills" of peculiar form. The weight of historic evidence seems to be in favor of the last derivation. Indeed, Johnson, in his "Wonder-working Providence," compared Beacon Hill, with its two hillocks, to the head and shoulders of a man, and therefore called the place Trea-mont; and William Wood, in his book called "New England's Prospect," printed in 1634, says, "To the north-west is a high mountain, with three little rising hills on the top of it; wherefore it is called Tramount." The same writer says of Boston, "His situation is very pleasant."

Fort Hill, Beacon and Copp's Hills were all distinguished in our colonial history. On Fort Hill, Andros, the tyrant governor under James II., was imprisoned, "bound in chains or cords," in the castle built there about 1640, until he was sent home to England. This ragged cliff, as it then appeared, commanded the harbor. It was anciently called Corn Hill, and was once the site of an Indian fort.

Beacon Hill was in the form of a sugar loaf, 138 feet in height from the water; on the summit was a tall, stout mast, secured by supporters, with treenail steps, and a barrel of tar on the top, forming a beacon. In times of danger this was guarded by a sentinel, ready to light it at a moment's alarm. From this circumstance it was called at first Sentry Hill. The view from this height was very extensive. The beacon to which it owes its permanent name was blown down in a violent storm in November, 1789; and the year following, a Doric column of brick and stone, sixty feet high, surmounted by a large gilt eagle, was erected under a subscription by the Bostonians. On the four sides of the pedestal, some of the leading events of the revolution were inscribed upon marble slabs; — the stamp act when passed and repealed, — the destruction of the tea, — battles of Lexington, Bunker Hill, Saratoga, and surrender at Yorktown, — and the confederation, independence, peace, and forming the constitution were among the subjects commemorated. For several years this column stood as a proud monument of glory, until taken down and the mountain where it stood levelled to enlarge the narrow territory of the growing place.

Beacon Hill was conveyed by the town of Boston to John Hancock, Esq., by deed, August 6, 1811. The lot is described in the deed as six rods square. It was bounded east and west by Bowdoin and Hancock Streets, and north and south by Mount Vernon and Derne Streets; and had Temple Street been laid out at that time, it would have run directly over the brow of this hill, and included the monument; which may give the stranger and the young of this day a more accurate idea of the locality of this eminence; for every feature of its position is now utterly effaced. Stately houses and handsome streets occupy or surround its site, once so memorable as a watch-tower. But the monument, with its pictorial features and historic inscriptions, still exists, recorded in the page of our country's annals, which neither frost, nor rain, nor the innovations of modern improvement can efface — *a convincing argument of the benefit which a humble work, like this, on Copp's Hill Burying-ground may render to other times.*

It may be well to remark, that Mr. Hancock caused the monument to be removed soon after the execution of his deed from the town, as he himself informed the writer of this introduction. The marble slabs and the gilt eagle were excepted in the purchase. The four slabs were deposited in a recess on the ground floor at the north-eastern part of the State House, where they are annexed to the wall. They are four feet four inches long, by three feet three inches wide. The eagle has been placed over the speaker's chair in the Hall of the Representatives; and there may this mute but national emblem of our glory excite all hearts to preserve our Union inviolate and forever.

Copp's Hill, in 1630, is thus described by Dr. Snow in his HISTORY OF BOSTON, p. 105: "The hill at the north, rising to the height of about fifty feet above the sea, presented there on its north-west brow an abrupt declivity, long after known as Copp's Hill steeps. Its summit, almost level, extended between Prince and Charter Streets towards Christ's Church. Thence south a gentle slope led to the water, which washed the south side of Prince Street below, and the north side above Thacher

Street as far as Salem Street. Eastward from the church, a gradual descent led to the North Battery, which was considered the bottom of the hill. South-easterly the slope was still more gradual, and terminated at the foot of the North Square, leaving a knoll on the right, where at present stands the meeting-house of the Second Church."

Copp's Hill rose gradually from Hudson's Point, so called from William Hudson, who owned it in 1635. This point and part of the hill were once the property of Joshua Gee, and Gee's noted shipyard lay at the foot of the hill northerly, a short distance from his house in Prince Street. It was afterwards used for a fortification, and called the North Battery. On the hill, Admiral Graves raised a battery of six guns and howitzers, and opened a fire on the American works in Charlestown, on the 17th of June, 1775. Charlestown was set on fire by bomb-shells thrown from this height, and by a body of marines, who landed in the easterly part of that town from the Somerset frigate. The scene has been described by writers with terrific splendor, while the battle of Bunker Hill was kindling that blaze of glory which finally triumphed in the deliverance of an oppressed people, and in the foundation of a great empire.

The first burying-ground, as it is said, laid out in Boston, was the King's Chapel Cemetery; for in the south-west corner of it, Isaac Johnson, the owner of a large tract there, was buried at his particular request. "He was a prime man among us, and made a godly end," Governor Winthrop remarked. Indeed, he was the principal founder of Boston — the fidus Achates of Winthrop, and was looked up to by him and the colonists as a guide. Mr. Johnson was the happy partner of Lady Arbella, whose early and untimely death was deeply lamented. He followed her September 30, 1629, before the name of *Tri-moun-tain* was changed to *Boston*, which was September 7, 1630.

Copp's Hill Burying-ground was the second place of interment. It was purchased by the town for this purpose in 1659. The spot was originally owned by William Copp. On the hill once stood a windmill, which, in August, 1632, was removed from Watertown, because "it would not grind with a westerly wind." It was called from this circumstance Windmill Hill, and afterwards took the name of Snow's Hill; eventually Copp's Hill, from William Copp, became its permanent name. Mr. Copp's realty is thus recorded, page 15, in the "Original Book of Possessions" of the town of Boston, now kept in the archives of the city at the City Hall.

"The possession of William Copp within the Limits of Boston. One house and lott of halfe an Acre in the Mill pond bounded wth Thomas Buttolph south-east: John Button northeast: the marsh on the south-west: and the River on the northwest."

The above is not dated, but there is reason to believe it was entered in 1644.

In the Probate Office for the county of Suffolk, there is a record of the will of William Copp, cordwainer. It was dated October 31, 1662, and proved April 27, 1670. Among the items of bequest are the following: "I give to my daughter Ruth my great kettle, little pot and chaffen dish." — "I give to Lydia my little kettle and great pot." In the inventory is a line appraising "1 hour glass and frying pan, 12 shillings." The amount of the inventory was almost £110 — no contemptible sum nearly two centuries ago.

Copp's Hill was formerly claimed by the Ancient and Honorable Artillery Company under a mortgage, which was finally discharged. Shaw, in his "Description of Boston," published in 1817, says that Mr. Copps was an elder in Dr. Mather's church; but erroneously, for he had several children, and it was his eldest son David who filled that office. His wife's name, Judith, is spelt Goodeth on the gravestone, and also in his will.

The foregoing origin of the name of Copp's Hill agrees with Snow's and Shaw's statements; but in the "History of the Ancient and Honorable Artillery Company," by Zachariah G. Whitman, is the following sentence, where he speaks of Nicholas Upshall: "Close beside him lay the gravestones of his wife

Dorothy and friend Obadiah Copp, from whom the hill is named." This must be the blunder of a careless compiler. Yet it shows how little is known of the man whose name is immortalized by this hill, where so many illustrious patriarchs sleep.

Since the appearance of Copp's Hill in 1630, as described by Dr. Snow, the features of the place have undergone a great change. Houses, streets, and wharves environ it; and the only open space is an area of about three acres, forming the cemetery, and including a lot of half an acre or more, bought by the town in 1806, and separated from the original burying-ground by a handsome granite wall. The whole is surrounded by a high, durable, and ornamental fence of iron. The grounds have been laid out in regular alleys and gravel paths, and embellished with a great variety of native forest-trees, some of which are of stately growth. The gravestones of many generations have been raised up, and numerous seats located under shady branches, where the aged and weary may pause, and the mourner find a quiet resting-place. Yet it is to be lamented, that the mounds and hillocks of the dead have been cut down to an unnatural level, and so many stones misplaced to form a geometrical row on the borders of the paths. This mode of restoring and adorning an ancient churchyard is singular ; and to speak of it kindly, and not in anger, it certainly was not the act of good taste.

This cemetery is now bounded north by Charter Street, west by Snow Hill Street, and south by Hull Street; the east is bordered by blocks of handsome brick houses, which shut out the picturesque view of the harbor, so attracting in olden time. Indeed, this airy spot, once so rich in scenery, is almost enclosed by buildings. Some years ago, the western margin was cut down nearly twenty feet, and a perpendicular wall erected, making the eastern border of Snow Hill Street. Formerly, before this side was dug down, there was a small rise of the land to the west of some seven feet higher. This formed the brow of an eminence with a very steep and abrupt bank to the

shore. From this lofty height the prospect of the harbor,
Charles River, and adjacent country must have been expansive
and magnificent. Here the British threw up a small fort and
erected a battery, from which they directed their fatal shells
in the burning of Charlestown.

At the north and north-west there is an open space, through
which part of Charlestown heights and the Navy Yard are visible;
and by taking a stand a little east from the western boundary,
the majestic OBELISK on Bunker Hill becomes visible, looming
up in solitary grandeur, and bringing to mind the words of the
GREAT ORATOR, when the corner stone of this monument was
laid by the Grand Lodge of Massachusetts, June 17, 1825:
"Let it rise! let it rise! till it shall meet the sun in its coming — let the earliest light of the morning gild it, and the parting day linger and play on its summit!"

In the vicinity of the burying-ground, about seventy yards
eastwardly from the south-east corner, is Christ Church, the
corner stone of which was laid April 15, 1723. A chime of
eight bells was added in 1744. Under it is a cemetery of
thirty-three tombs. The venerable Dr. Eaton, formerly rector of
this church, in a discourse delivered December 28, 1823, gives
an interesting history of its origin, and relates an anecdote
somewhat singular: the sprigs of evergreen I have Italicized.

"The following fact, which in some ages would have excited
the superstitious veneration of ignorance and bigotry, may be
worth recording. Some years since, in 1812, while the work-
men were employed in the cemetery building tombs, one of
them found the earth so loose that he settled his bar into it the
whole length with a single effort. The superintendent directed
him to proceed till he found solid earth. About six feet below
the bottom of the cellar he found a coffin covered with a coarse
linen cloth, sized with gum, which on boiling became white,
and the texture as firm as if it had been recently woven.
Within this coffin was another, protected from the air in a similar manner, and the furniture was not in the least injured by
time. The flesh was sound, and somewhat resembling that of

an Egyptian mummy. The skin, when cut, appeared like leather. *The sprigs of evergreen, deposited in the coffin,* resembled the broad-leaved myrtle ; the stem was elastic, the leaves fresh, and apparently in a state of vegetation. From the inscription it was found to be the body of Mr. Thomas, a native of New England, who died in Bermuda. Some of his family were among the founders of Christ Church. His remains, when discovered, had been entombed about eighty years. They now rest in the north-east corner of the cemetery, and the stone so long concealed from observation is placed over them." — *Shaw,* p. 259, note.

Dr. William Walter officiated as rector of this church from 1792 to 1800, of whose death Bishop Samuel Parker, D. D., of Trinity Church, who died in 1804, remarked, that "religion mourns the loss of one of her most obedient children and brightest ornaments." It is worthy of observation that in Christ Church was the first monument ever erected to the memory of Washington in America. Shaw * describes it, " at the east end of the church on the side of the chancel, with a bust well executed by an Italian artist."

The steeple of this church commands a rich prospect. It is said that Governor Gage ascended here to gaze at the conflagration of Charlestown, and the battle of Bunker Hill.

The cemetery on Copp's Hill was much injured during the revolutionary war. From an adjacent battery the soldiers used some of the gravestones for targets, mutilated others, whenever

---

* Charles Shaw, Esq., author of the " History of Boston," was born in Bath, Maine, and took his degree at Harvard University, 1805, with the second part in his class and a high reputation as a scholar. He studied law with Nathaniel Coffin, Esq., of Bath, practised some years in Jefferson, Lincoln county, and afterwards went to Montgomery, in Alabama, where he was appointed a judge, and died. He was a man of elegant taste, excelled in his knowledge of the Latin language, — being, it was said, among the uncommonly few who could scan Horace with a musical cadence. Though a poet and a fine writer, he only left this little work *in memoriam.*

a patriotic epitaph thereon excited their ire or envy, and took
many to pave the hospital for their invalids. But the worst
enemy to the memory of the dead — disgraceful as it may appear — was among our own citizens. For within a few years,
some of the slabs — solemnly inscribed as they were — individ-
uals carried off with impunity to cover drains, make foundations
for chimneys, lay at the bottom of tombs for coffins to rest on,
or at their mouths to close up the aperture.

There was a period in the burial history of our country which
reflects no honor on a Christian land ; especially when we remember that the Hebrews, Greeks, and Romans, and even the
Turks, in their cypress-planted cemeteries, ever honored the
ashes of the dead. It seemed not enough to erect temples to
God, without regard to any order of architecture, without
form or comeliness, looking like steepled barns, and then
to use them for unholy purposes and town meetings ; but,
in too many instances, the very churchyards were neg-
lected, unfenced and uncared for, the graves exposed to
horses, cattle, and dogs, not a tree nor a flower suffered to
shade or bloom there, and neither walk nor path laid out among
the falling, straggling stones, for the pensive mourner to muse
over a loved one, or drop a tear over his grave. The sexton
appeared to be the only frequent visitant to the spot; the first
with his spade and pick to disturb the solitude of the scene
after the funeral procession had buried the dead out of their
sight and gone home. This is no colored nor fanciful description of hundreds of village churchyards, within twenty years
past, on the hills and in the valleys of New England. Are
there not, even at this day, such desecrated spots of burial in
some of our neighboring cities? Let Worcester and Roxbury
answer! If the manes of departed worth could speak from
their dishonored graves, they would envy even the fate of Pali-
nurus in his watery tomb, —

"Nudus in ignota, Palinure, jacebis arena."

But, thank Heaven, a change is coming over the land. It is

not in Mount Auburn alone, nor at Laurel Hill in Philadelphia, nor on Green Mount in Baltimore, nor in the Greenwood Cemetery in New York, nor in the time-honored churchyard at New Haven, where a more enlightened taste and holier feelings prevail. A degree of veneration is awakened, and a regard for the sanctuary of the grave is more generally felt in the busy world. We have begun to honor the ashes of the dead, and their memory is cherished from the simple green mound, adorned with shrubs and flowers, to the solid granite and architectural marble of the costly tomb. It soothes the heart of the mourner of refined feelings to think, when he walks in the valley of the shadow of death, that his beloved ones are not forgotten.

It is remarkable that, amidst such desecration of these ancient memorials on Copp's Hill, so many epitaphs escaped destruction, and can be identified; for in addition to losses thus sustained, very many gravestones have been removed, with the remains they guarded, to churchyards in distant places, there to be preserved with reverence.

A singular instance of depravity, however, did occur in Copp's Hill Burying-ground. Here once rested the bones of Thomas Hutchinson, — father of Governor Hutchinson, — one of the greatest benefactors of this city and country, and also the bones of his father Elisha, son of the famous Edward Hutchinson, who fell in an attack of the Indians at Quabaog, in Brookfield, and a descendant from the celebrated Ann and her husband, Governor William Hutchinson, of Rhode Island. Their bones are now scattered before the four winds of heaven! Their tomb has passed into the hands of strangers. Over their beautiful coat of arms their name has been *expunged*, and the name of Thomas Lewis inserted!

One would think that decency — if there were a drop of modest blood to curdle round the heart at such a thought-of baseness — would at least have discovered some veneration for our departed patriots, if the sanctuary of the tomb, which all nations have respected, had no influence. Even the poor Indian, by whom the sepulchral mounds in his fatherland have ever been regarded with the loftiest feelings of reverence, would have raised his tomahawk to cut off the sacrilegious hand which dared to violate the home of his honored dead.

An infamous custom has prevailed among some of the sextons in this city of *speculating in tombs.* Finding a poor widow, or dilapidated heir, having a share or fractional interest in some old tomb under his care, the grave-digger, aware of the absence or death of the principal owner, and that "a living dog is better than a dead lion," purchases it for a trifle, seizes the whole by prescription, or threats of the law, calls it his own, erases the family name, clears out the sacred relics which lie there, and then makes a trade of his *mortmain* right, by selling a berth for dead strangers in the city, at eight, or ten, or twelve dollars apiece, as the case may be. This has been repeatedly done on Copp's Hill, King's Chapel, and other burial-grounds in the city.

Nor is this all. After the tombs have been filled up by the remains of strangers, their corpses have been carted out of town in the night season, or buried in a hole dug at the bottom of the tomb, pounded down in one horrid, hideous mass, and covered over, to make way for more death-money. An aged gentleman of respectability, residing near Copp's Hill, told me he has seen loads of broken-up coffins removed from tombs thus desecrated; and a lady in this city recently remarked that within fifteen years she was in that cemetery, and there saw a collection of coffins heaped up for removal; on the fragments of one of which skin and hair adhered — the hair black and glossy — the long, fine hair of a female; and she shuddered and turned away from the spectacle!

In King's Chapel Burying-ground, there is a tomb on the north side, near a window of the room of the Massachusetts Historical Society, where the sexton, lately deceased, thus used it for speculation, erased the family name on the great brown stone tablet, and put his own in its place.

Such sacrilege is outrageous. It almost makes the blood boil with indignation. Is the law against profanity of the dead a mere spider's web, made by the weak to favor the wicked?

What would be the feelings of the tender mother, or affectionate daughter, in the days of their mourning, should it be told them, "The grave is no resting-place for the dead; the sacred ashes of a husband or father will one day be scattered by the hand of the sexton, and a greedy, unprincipled grave-digger will claim your ancestral tomb for a mere pittance, and turn it into a mercenary charnel-house to suit his purposes"?

If there be any doubt of the facts here stated, let the records of the Probate Office in Boston be searched for twenty years past. It will there be seen how many sextons have left a legacy of tombs in their will, as a profitable investment to their heirs. Names could be mentioned, but I forbear. Will not "A Sexton of the Old School" point his heavy artillery against this abomination? It ought to be investigated and denounced, so that no speculator in tombs and bones would dare to show his head among a church-going people. Let the city authorities look to this matter, and put a stop forever to a species of merchandise, next only to that of *Burking* for the dissecting room!

Copp's Hill Burying-ground is a locality full of reminiscences. It is pleasing to observe, that the city authorities have sought to preserve the garden of the dead, and put it under the care of a *faithful* person. It has been furnished with a Cochituate fountain, and has become a favorite place of promenade to citizens in the northern part of the city, remote from the refreshing walks of our beautiful Mall. It is worthy of the stranger's notice; more especially if he feel interested in the antiquities of this city. He will see tombs with heraldic insignia of other times carved on the tablets; those of Hutchinson, Mountford, Goodrich, Gee, Clark, Lee, and Greenwood will arrest his eye. Nor can he pass unobserved the venerable, time-touched sepulchres of those Reverend and revered men, Andrew and John Elliot, Increase, Cotton, and Samuel Mather, learned doctors of divinity, scholars of note and pastors of celebrity in their day, with whom the history of New England is, and forever will be, associated. Here their remains have long slept, unconscious of the thunders which shook this hill in 1775, and of the tread of thousands of visitors to this spot, and of the voices of many a playful school, which for nearly three generations of national prosperity have echoed near their silent mansion of death. Friend and foe, female loveliness and infantile beauty, here lie side by side; in a word, here is the dust of many a daring, lion-hearted, devout first settler in the town of Shawmut, now the expanding city of Boston.

He will see one gravestone where Grace Berry lies beneath, singularly shaped, and marked by the bullets of a British foe before the evacuation of Boston, when unholy hands used it for a target; in another spot is the slab, which designates the ashes of Nicholas Upshall, of the Ancient and Honorable Artillery, a public-spirited man, persecuted for religious opinions among a religious people; and a little farther off stands a memorial to Captain Thomas Lake, an early settler, and large proprietor in Maine, " an eminently faithful servant of God," who was slain by the Indians, at Kennebec, August 14, 1670.

While meditating among the tombs in this shady necropolis, he may observe in the south-west corner a large and stately monument of granite, over a capacious sepulchre, dedicated to seamen of all nations, by the Rev. Phineas Stowe, pastor of the First Baptist Bethel Church in Boston, 1851 — a generous and highly honorable testimony of respect to that noble and too little valued class of our citizens. And from this spot let him, as he muses from grave to grave along these gravelled walks, turn to the north-east angle of the cemetery, where he will see a marble pyramid over the tomb of Ellis, and by its side, within the iron railing, a wide-spread weeping willow. *Siste, viator.* Traveller, pause; for that willow casts no vulgar shade. It is an exotic. It grew up from a shoot taken from that lonely tree which hangs over the deserted grave of the great Napoleon at St. Helena; and it needs no poetry of the heart to feel, as we gaze upon the umbrage, as if every sea breeze from the eastern world touched its leaves with sorrow, and called forth a train of mournful reflections at the fate of that wonderful man!

The compiler of this book of Epitaphs has spared no pains to verify the facts he has published. He has sought the aged, and listened to their early recollections; he has caused many an old gravestone, buried beneath the sod, to be dug up and carefully examined; and he has *descended into vaults, and from thence brought up hidden treasures.* The work he has done will be valuable, because it will tend to perpetuate names and dates, which a few years more would render it difficult to resuscitate, and which the antiquary of another generation might explore in vain among the fugitive landmarks of tradition. What OLD MORTALITY accomplished with hammer and chisel on the tombstones of the Covenanters he has endeavored to perform with spade and pen.

He only asks encouragement as a reward of labors which the circumstances of his life forbid him, in justice to his family, to bestow gratuitously. Should this volume meet with the approbation of the liberal descendants, whose ancestral memorials he has attempted to preserve by the imperishable power of the press, he will soon offer to the public a similar work on King's Chapel Burying-ground — the materials of which are in a state of preparation.

The assistance kindly afforded him by John P. Bigelow, Esq., Mayor of Boston, he would gratefully acknowledge; and also that of many other gentlemen, — some of high standing, — whose names he would gladly mention; but a selection would seem invidious, and to enumerate them all might encroach upon the patience which this long, but he hopes not useless, preamble may have wearied.

BOSTON, August, 1851.

[The compiler is indebted to the kindness of JOHN H. SHEPPARD, Esq., for the valuable Introduction to this volume.]

List of Engravings.

VIEW OF COPP'S HILL, ... Frontispiece.

LAKE   COAT OF ARMS, ... Page 2

GREENWOOD   "   " 14

GOODRICH   "   " 60

MOUNTFORT   "   " 81

CLARK   "   " 102

MARTYN   "   " 125

MARINERS' TOMB, ... 128

GEE   COAT OF ARMS, ... 140

THORNTON   "   " 162

SNELLING   "   " 214

LORING   "   " 221

MONUMENT TO MAJOR GENERAL JOSEPH WARREN, . 233

      "   " THE APOSTLE ELIOT, ... 252

Inscriptions

FROM

Copp's Hill Burial Ground.

```
┌─────────────────┐
│  MATHER         │
│  TOMB.          │
└─────────────────┘
```

THE REVERE** DOCTORS
INCREASE, COTTON,
& SAMUEL MATHER
were intered in this Vault

'TIS the TOMB OF our FATHER'S
MATHER CROER'S**

I DIED Augt 27th 1723 Æ 84
C DIED FEB 13th 1727 Æ 65
S DIED JUNE 27$^{.h}$ 1785 Æ 79

JOANNA DAUGHT
OF WILLIAM & ANNE COPP
AGED
6 MONTHES DIED
MARCH y^e 20
162$\frac{5}{6}$

CAP^T THOMAS LAKE
AGED 61 YEERES
AN EMINENTLY FAITHFVLL SERVANT
OF GOD & ONE OF A PVBLIC SPIRIT
WAS PERFIDIOVSLY SLAIN BY
y^e INDIANS AT KENNIBECK
AVGVST y^e 14th 1676
& HERE INTERED THE 13 OF
MARCH FOLLOWING.

Here lyeth ye body of
JOHN LAKE
Son to Capt. Thomas Lake
Aged abovt 24 years
Deceased ye 27 of Iune
1 6   9 0

> **HOOTON & WATTS'**
> **TOMB.**

Deacon
I O H N   P H I L L I P E S
Aged 77 yeares
Deceased
the 16 day of December
1 6 8 2

The   2
1 6   8 0
HEZEKIAH HARES
aged 1 year 11 mo deced ye 31 of January
JOHN HARES
age 9 months dece^d ye 23 of August
1 6 7 4

Here lyes buried
the Body of
C A P^T   R A L P H   H A R T T
Who departed this life
the 14th of March
1 7 7 6
Aged 77 years

& HANNAH HARES

CHILDREN OF WM.

JOHN yᵉ Son of
JOHN & ANNABEL SALISBURY
Died December yᵉ 15 1704 in yᵉ
14 year of his age.

ELIZABETH
wife to NICHLAS SALSBVRY
aged 53 years departed
this life yᵉ 17 of February
1 6 8 $\frac{7}{8}$

ELIZABETH	Here lyeth yᵉ Body
late wife	of
GEORGE ROBINSON	THOMAS LUSCOMB
aged about 40 Years	aged about 35 Years
deceased	decᵈ
yᵉ 7ᵗʰ of July	October yᵉ 15
1 6 9 7	1 6 9 4

Here lyeth buried yᵉ Body of
GRACE BERRY
yᵉ Wife of
Thomas Berry
Age about 58 Years who died May yᵉ 17
1 6 2 5

Memento Mori Fugit Hora
Here
Lyes the Body of
N A T H A N A E L   A D A M S
Aged 60 Years
Deceased the 29ᵗʰ of March
1 6 8 $\frac{9}{90}$

* * re lyeth buried
* ody of
ELIZABETH *EARE
Relict of
* ILLIAM WEARE
Aged 90 Years dec^d y^e 27 of September
1 6 8 1

IOHANA PHILLIPES
the Wife of IOHN PHILLIPES
Aged 80 Yeares
deceased y^e 22 of October 1 6 7 5

Here lyeth bvrie^d the Body of
IOHN SAXTON
Aged 38 Years departed
this Life the 31 day of
IVLY 1686

1 6 7 7
A B I G A I L   A Y R E S
AGED 27 YEARS DYED ye 2
OF JANWARY

ELIZABETH CHAPIN
ye Daughter of
EBENEZER & ELIZABETH CHAPIN
Aged about 16 m°
Died August ye 23 1694

ELIZABETH SHUTE
aged 1 Week
Dyed ye 2 Febvar 1 6 6 5

1 *

MICHAEL POWELL
aged 67 Yeares
Desesed the 28 of December
1 6 7 2

LYDIA BROUN
Wife to WILLIAM BROUN
aged about 46 Years
dec^d July ye 30
1 6 8 0

ISAAC GRIFFIN
aged about 55
Years died
July ye 29 1693

SARAH RULE
aged 9 Years
died
July ye 5 1690

ELIZABETH
Daughter of JOHN & ELIZABETH PICKERIN
Aged 16 m°
Died August y^e 27
1 6 9 0

Here lyeth buried y^e Body of
EDWARD GRANT
Aged about 50 Years dec^d y^e 19th day of June
1 6   8 2

ALES HOWARD
Relict of
LEFT^T WILLIAM HOWARD
Aged 72 Years
dec^d Nov y° 18
1 6 8 1

Here lyes the Body of
EXPERIENCE MILES
Aged 49 Years dec[d]
January the 26
1 6 * $\frac{0}{1}$

WILLIAM TYER
Aged 26 Years
died
Iavaryy 14
1 6 6 6

MARTHA HASEY
Aged 12 Yeares
dyed
the 4th of May
1 6 7 6

REBEKAH HOOPER
the Davghter of GORG HOOPER
Aged
2 Yeares & 10 Weeks
Dyed the 15 of October 1 6 7 5

Here lyeth buried
y[e] Body of
ALEXANDER ADAMS
Aged 62 years dyed y[e] 15th day of January
1 6 7 7

NATHANIEL SAXTON
Aged 19 Years dyed y[e] 15 of September
1 6 7 7

Here lyeth buried y[e] Body of
MARY BULL
Wife to JAMES BULL
Aged about 75 yeares died y[e] 29 of Aug[ust]
1 6 8 8

LYDIA HOUGH
Wife to WILLIAM HOUGH
Aged 38 years dec^d y^e 26th day of February
1 6 8 $\frac{2}{3}$

CHARLES FARNUM
Aged
3 years & 6 m
Dec^d
January y^e 21 – 1 6 7 $\frac{7}{8}$

Here lyeth buried
y^e Body of
WILLIAM KENT
Aged 57 years dec^d
June y^e 9th 1 6 9 1

In Memorial of
DORATHY VPSHALL
Aged 73 Yeares deceased the 18 of September
1 6 7 5

ANNAH READE
Wife to Obadiah Reade aged 33 years
Dyed y^e 13 day of September
1 6 8 0

Here lyes the Body of
FRANSIS WARD
Wife to SAMUEL WARD
Aged 83 Years dyed the 10th of Ivne
1 6 9 0

Here lyeth buried ye Body of
MARY WINSLOW
Daughter to Mr. Samuel Winslow
Aged 3 years
Departed this life June ye 2^d
1 6 8 1

Here lyes the Body of
JOHN PITTOM
Aged about 54 Years died February 30th (?)
1 6 9 9

THE 3 CHILDREN OF OBADIAH & ELIZABETH GILL

Obadiah Gill	Obadiah Gill	Samuel Gill
aged	aged	aged
7 months & 1	6 months	3 years & 7
half	dyed	months
dyed ye 9 day of	ye 3 of	dyed ye 6 day of
August	July	June
1 6 8 2	1 6 7 8	1 6 7 9

Here lyeth buried ye Body of
R I C H A R D   C O L L A C O T T
Aged 83 years
Dyed July ye 7
1 6 8 6

MARY HUNTING
ye daughter of
SAMUEL & MARY HUNTING
Aged 13 months & 25 days
Died July ye 29
1 6 9 9

Here lyeth ye Body of
J O H N   M A V E R I C K E
Son of
JOHN & MRS ELIZABETH MAVERICKE
Who died July 17 1734 aged
10 years & 6 m°

Here lyes buried the Body of
MRS MARY GILBURT Relict of
Capt Thomas Gilburt
aged 63 years
Dec^d Decm^r ye 30th

MRS. SARAH SHAW
1 7 9 9

JACOB HALL'S TOMB.

Here lies intered the
mortal part of
MR JOHN ADAMS
who departed
this life
March ye 1st 1783
Æ 67 years

Here lieth buried
ye Bodi of
OBODIAH GILL
Deacon of y^e
North Church in Boston
Aged 50 years decesed
January ye 6–1700

Here lyes ye Body of
MRS MEHITABEL MAVERICKE
Wife of Mr Jotham Mavericke
Aged 24 years dyed
June 30th 1 7 4 7

Here lyeth buried y^e
Body of
JOSEPH SHAW SENIER
Aged 56 years died
May ye 7th
1 7 0 1

Sacred to the Memory of
MR JACOB HAWKINS
Who professed faith in Jesus Christ about 14
Years & about 1 year a Preacher of the
Gospel. He was one of a sound Judg-
ment meek & happy Spirit. He
ended his days in peace
July 10th 1797 aged 31 years.

EDWARD CARNES'
TOMB.

In Memory of	In Memory of
MR JOSHUA BOWLES	MRS MARY BOWLES
who	Wife of
died Augst 31	Mr Joshua Bowles who
1794	died Janry 16
Ætat 72	1780 Ætat 52

" Blessed are the dead which die in the Lord."

Here
lyes ye Body of
MRS HANNAH STODDARD
Wife to
Mr After Stoddard
Who died December ye 29th
1755

Here lyes buried the Body of
MR JOSIAH CLARK
Who decd August the 27th 1726 aged
45 year

Reader
Beneath this Stone is deposited the Remains of
MAJOR THOMAS SEWARD
Who gallantly fought in our late
REVOLUTIONARY WAR
And through its various Scenes behaved
With Patriotic Fortitude and
Died in the Calms of domestic Felicity as
becomes a universal Christian
November 27th 1800
Ætat 60

" The lonely turf where silence lays her head,
The mound where pity sighs for hond dead,
Such is the grief where sorrow now doth sigh,
To learn to live is but to learn to die."

Also
SARAH SEWARD his Wife
Obiit March 14th 1800
Ætat 63

Here lies buried in
A stone grave 10 feet deep
CAPT DANIEL MALCOM MERCHT
Who departed this life
October 23d
1 7 6 9
Aged 44 years
A true Son of Liberty a Friend to the Public
An Enemy to Oppression and One of
the foremost in opposing the
Revenue Acts on
America

Here lyes ye Body of
M^{RS} MARY HARTT Wife to
Mr Ralph Hartt
Aged
34 years and 2 mo dec^d
Agust ye 2^d
1 7 3 3

Here lyes buried ye Body of
MRS LOIS HARTT
The Wife of Capt Ralph Hartt
Aged 46 years deceased
Novr 5th 1 7 5 1

Mr George Worthy Lake | Ruth Worthy Lake
1 7 1 8 | 1 7 1 8
Mrs Ann Worthy Lake
1 7 1 8

ELIZABETH late Wife
George Robinson
Aged about 40 years deceased ye 7th of July
1 6 9 7

Here lyes buried y^e Body of
M^{RS} MARY THACHER Widdow
late Wife of Judah Thatcher of Yarmouth
departed this life Novr y^e 30 1708
in y^e 68th year of her age

Here lyes y^e Body of
MR FRANCES HUDSON
aged 55 years dec^d
June y^e 13 1 7 3 2

GREENWOOD

Here lyeth intered the Body of
NATHANIEL GREENWOOD
Aged 53 years
Departed this life July the 31
1 6 8 4

Here lyes buried yᵉ Body of
DAUID COPP
Elder of yᵉ Old Church in Boston
Aged 78 years decᵈ
November the 20
1 7 1 3

Here lyes y^e Body of
HARVEY THOMAS
Aged 39 years who departed this life
Sept y^e 12th 1 7 5 0

Here lyes y^e Body of
MR THOMAS DELAPLACE
Died Decr y^e 25th 1733 in y^e 60th year of his age

Here lyes the Body of
MRS MARY CONEY
Who died Jan^{ry} y^e 30th 1 7 4 9 $-\frac{1}{50}$ aged
80 years

Here lyes buried y^e Body of
MR NATHANIE AYRES
aged 67 years & 6 m^o dec^d
December y^e 4th
1 7 3 1

Here lyes buried y^e Body of
MRS SARAH WALES
Wife to Mr Timothy Wales dec^d May y^e 3^d
1 7 2 6
in ye 57th year of her age

Here lyes y^e Body of
HANNAH GREEN
Wife to
John Green Cen^r
Aged 63 years & about 4 m^o
Died January y^e 3^d
1 7   1 7 $\frac{1}{18}$

Here lies y^e Body of
MRS ABIGAIL FURBUR the Wife of
Mr Richard Furbur
Who died July y^e 11th
1 7 5 0
Aged 33 years

Here lyes buried
The Body of CAPT WILLIAM DOWRICK
aged 38 years & 3 m^o died
March y^e 10th 1748$\frac{}{9}$

Here lyes y^e	Here lyes y^e
Body of	Body of
HANNAH SHUTT	MRS MARY SHUTT
Daughter of	the Wife of
Capt Michael and Mrs	Capt Michael Shutt
Mary Shutt aged	aged
16 years and 8 months	45 years and eight months
who deceased	who deceased
April the 29th	September the 16th
1 7 0 9	1 7 0 9

Here lyeth Buried y^e Body of
JOHN GREEN Senior
aged 59 years
Died February y^e 25
1 7 0 $\frac{1}{2}$

Here lies the Body of
MRS ELIZABETH AUSTILL
Wife of Capt Joseph Austill
Who died June y^e 18th 1 7 6 7
In the 80 year of her age

Here lies buried the Body of
MRS REBECCA CLARKE Widow of
Mr John Clark
Aged 82 years died
Jan^{ry} 2^d
1 7 6 3

Here lyes the Body of
M E H E T E B E L   S C A R L E T
Wife to Mr Humphrey Scarlet
Dec^d June ye 26th
1 7 3 3
In ye 43^d year of her age

Here	Here
lies the body of	lyes buried the body of
MRS MARY WATSON	MR JAMES WATSON
wife of	dec^d
CAPT JAMES WATSON	July ye 22^d 1738
aged 59 years died	in y^e
Oct 1st 1 7 4 3	58th year of his age

Here lyeth buried ye Body of
MR JOSEPH BUCKLEY
Aged
42 years and 6 mounthes
Died Jan ye 1
1 7 0 1

Here lyeth buried
ye Body of JOSEPH GLIDDEN
aged about 32 years
Died Noue^r ye 24 1 7 0 0

Here lyes buried yᵉ Body of
MRS MARTHA PEARSON
formerly yᵉ wife of
Mᴿ JOHN GOODWIN
Aged 76 years who departed this life
Sept yᵉ 26 1 7 2 8

Here lyes buried
the Body of JOHN GOODWIN
aged 65 years
departed this life June yᵉ 21ˢᵗ
1 7 1 2

Here lyes buried
yᵉ Body of MRS MARY GOODWIN
aged 85 years died July yᵉ 16ᵗʰ
1 7 5 9

Here lyes yᵉ Body of
DORCAS BALLARD Wife to
Daniel Ballard aged
about 57 years died June yᵉ 22ᵈ 1 7 1 9

Here lyes yᵉ Body of
ABIGAIL COOPER Wife of
Edward Cooper died
March yᵉ 11ᵗʰ 1718 in the 31ˢᵗ year of her age

Here lyes buried yᵉ Body of
MRS HANNAH WOODBURY Wife to
Mr Andrew Woodbury
Who departed this life July 28ᵗʰ
1 7 3 3
* * yᵉ 37ᵗʰ year of her age

JEREMIAH MERRILLS
Aged about 70 years dec^d August y^e 25
1 7 1 9

Here lyeth y^e Body of
SUSANNAH WADSWORTH
y^e Wife of Timothy Wadsworth
Dec^d April y^e 3^d 1 7 0 4
in y^e 37th year of her age

Here lyes buried y^e Body of
C A P T R I C H A R D H A R R I S
aged about 63 years who
dec^d March y^e 10th
1 7 1 3 $_{14}$

Here lieth y^e Body of
MICHAEL NOWEL aged about 33 years
Died Aug y^e 27th
1 6 9 6

Here lies y^e Body of
R E B A C C A
Wife to OBADIAH WARFIELD
aged 38 years
died May the 28
1 7 1 5

Here lyes buried the Body of
MR DEAN GROVER
Aged 46 Years
dec^d
August 15 1 7 3 4

Here lyes buried y^e Body of
MR ROBERT SEARES
who departed this life Decem^{br} 29th 1 7 3 2
in ye 76 year of his age

Here lyes ye Body of
ABIGAIL THOMAS
Wife to
William Thomas
dec^d May ye 4th 1717
in the 33^d year of her age

SACRED
To the Memory of
MR PAUL FARMER
who died December 26th
1 7 9 1
aged 77 years

Here lyes ye Body of
WILLIAM MUMFORD
aged 77 years died Novr ye 21st
1 7 1 8

In Memory of
MR THOMAS CHRISTY
who died Octr 21st
1 7 9 8
aged 62 years

Here lyes ye Body of
MRS ABIGAIL INGHAM late Wife of
Mr North Ingham who dec^d
April ye 10th 1 7 2 8
in ye 36th year of her age

Here lyeth intered
The Body of MICHAEL MARTYN
aged 60 years dec^d March ye 26
1 6 8 2

In Memory of
MRS MARGARET CLARK
the virtuous consort of
Capt Joseph Clark
She died Jany 11th 1761
Ætat 69

Here lyes ye Body of
MR JOSEPH HOOD
aged 55 years
dec^d December ye 14th
1 7 2 9

In Memory of
MR JOSEPH CLARK
died Oct 16th 1783
aged
67 years

Here lyeth ye Body of
ELIZABETH Wife of William Greenough
* * * * *   * * * *

In Memory of
MRS PRUDENCE CLARK
Widow of
Mr Joseph Clark
deceased 13 December
1 7 8 9
aged 68 years

Here lyes ye Body of
MRS SARAH CLARK Wife of
Mr Samuel Clark died
August 9 1799 aged 56 years

Here lyes the Body of
MRS HANNAH CLARK the Wife of
Mr Samuel Clark
who died Feb 13 1764 aged 35 years

Here lyes ye Body of
MR WILLIAM HOUGH
aged 67 years died November ye 8th
1 7 1 4

Here lyes ye Body of
J O H N   R U S S E L L
who departed this life September y^e 28th
1 7 0 9

Here lyes buried y^e Body of
M R   W I L L I A M   B U R R O U G H
aged about 70 years dec^d
April y^e 21st **1 7 1 1**

Here lyes y^e Body of
MRS MARY ATTWOOD Wife to
Deacon John Atwood
aged
68 years dec^d March y^e 18th
1 7 2 8 $_9$

Here lyes y^e Body of
S A R A H
y^e daughter of William & Sarah Clark
aged 18 months died August 5
1   7   0   4

Here lyes buried
The Body of **MR THADEUS SARGENT**
Son to
Mr Thomas Sargent
died y^e 26th of January **1 7 7 3**
in the 37th year of his age

Here lyeth buried
The Body of MRS MARY HICKS
Wife of Mr Zachariah Hicks
aged 49 years who died
December y[e] 30th
1 7 4 7

Here lyes buried y[e] Body of
MRS ELIZA FIFIELD
Widow of
Capt Giles Fifield
aged 84 years who died June y[e] 16th 1 7 4 3

Here lyes y[e] Body of
MRS ABIGAIL STODDARD Wife to
Capt Thomas Stoddard
and daughter of Mr Benjamin Barker of Andover
who died July 23[d] 1 7 6 1
in y[e] 60th year of her age

Here lies the Body of
CAPT THOMAS STODDARD
who departed this life
April the 12th 1763 in y[e] 64th year of his age

Here lyes the Body of
CAPT WILLIAM TROUT
Died March 31st 1 7 4 2
in y[e] 53[d] year of his age

ELIZABETH PEIRSE
Dau[r] to Moses & Elizabeth Peirse
aged 7 years died Nov y[e] 1st
1 7 2 1

Erected to the Memory of
MRS PATIENCE CAPEN
the consort of
Mr Hopestill Capen
who died Jan 19th 1791
aged 57 years

Here lyes the body of
MRS ELIZTH STODDARD Wife to
Mr Daniel Stoddard &
dau^r to Mr John & Elizth Ballard
aged 70 year dec^d
Feb^{ry} y^e 20th 1732

Here lyes the Body of
S A M U E L
Son of SAMUEL & MARY GREENWOOD
aged near 34 years died Dec y^e 10
1 7 1 1

Here lyes y^e Body of
M A R Y
y^e wife to John Pittom aged 69 years died
March y^e 17th 1 7 $\frac{12}{13}$

Here lyes y^e Body of
SAMUEL GREENWOOD
aged about 65 years died
y^e 19 of August
1 7 1 1

Here lyes y^e Body of
EDWARD RANSFORD
aged 48 years died Dec the 27th
1 7 1 7

Here lyes y[e] Body of
MRS MARY SCOTT Widdow of
Capt John Scott
aged 87 years died Nov[r] 23[d]
1 7 5 4

Here lyes buried
the body of
MRS ELIZABETH KENNEY
died May 6th
1 7 5 3 aged 65 years

Here lyes the Body of
MR RICHARD JONES
aged 28 years
dec[d] Dec y[e] 8th
1 7 3 1

Here lies buried the Body of
MRS HANNAH WHITE Widdow of
Capt Samuel White aged 73 years
Dec[d] Dec[r] y[e] 9th
1 7 3 6

Here lyes y[e] Body of
NATHANIEL GILL aged 30 years & 7 mo
deceased Oct y[e] 3[d]
1 7 2 0

Here lies the Body of
MISS HANNAH LANGFORD Daugh[r] of
Mr Nicholas & Mrs Joanna Langford
who died Nov[r] 19th 1796
aged
15 years & 6 months

" Nor youth nor inocence could save
Hannah, from the insatiable grave,
But cease our tears no longer weep
The little maid doth only sleep
Anon she'll wake & rise again
And in her Savours Arms remain."

Here lyes ye Body of
MR JAMES PULLINGTON
aged 51 years dec^d June the 11th 1 7 3 5

Here lyes the Body of
CAPT JOSEPH BUCKLEY
who departed this life January the 2^d
1 7 6 4
aged 32 years

Sacred to the Memory of
MISS JOANNA BUCKLEY who died
Jan 3^d 1 8 0 2 Æ 64

Blessed are the dead who die in the Lord

In Memory of
MR GERSHOM WHITTEMORE
son of Mr Thomas & Mrs Anna Whittemore
who died Nov 1st 1 7 9 5
aged 20 years

Here lyes buried the Body of
MR JOHN WATERHOUSE
aged 37 years died Jan ye 1st
1 7 4 6

Here lies ye Body of
MR LEONARD BARRONS
Son to
Mr John and Mrs Mary Barrons of
Salcombregis in Devon, died
Oct 25th 1 7 6 5 aged
33 years

Here lyes buried
The Body of MR ELIAS PARKMAN
aged 52 years 5 mo & * * daye
dec^d May the 24th 1 7 4 1

Here lyes buried
The *ody of MRS ELIZABETH PARKMAN
wife to Mr Elias Parkman who died
Nov y^e 1st 1 7 4 6 in the 58th
year of her age

This Stone perpetuates the Memory of
DOC ELIAS PARKMAN
Who departed this life March y^e 6th
1 7 5 0 — aged 33

Here lyes y^e Body of
ELIZABETH Wife to Obadiah Read
aged 67 years
died Feb^{ry} 26th 1 7 1 2 $_{13}$

Here lyes the Body of
M R   J A M E S   B A R T E R
aged 71 years died May 16th 1 7 5 7

Here lyes the Body of
MR EDWARD EDES aged 49 years
dec^d Sep y^e 28th
1 7 3 *

Here lies buried
The Body of MR JOHN CLOUGH
died July y^e 6 1 7 5 6
aged 46 years

In Memory of MRS MARY STEVENS
Wife to Mr Thomas Stevens who
departed this life May 9th
1 7 8 5
in the 75th year of her age
Blessed are the dead that die in the Lord for they rest from
their labours & their works do follow them

Here lies the Body of
SARAH STEVENS Wife to
Thomas Stevens aged
about 52 years dec d Nov y e 30
1 7 2 3

Here lies the Body of
MR THOMAS STEUENS
died May 6th
1 7 6 1

Here lyes buried the Body of
MR SAMUEL GOFFE dec d Sep the 11th
1 7 4 0
in the 58th year of his age

Here lyes buried the Body of
CAPT THOMAS PORTER
dec d April y e 11th
1 7 3 8
in the 63d year of his age

Here lyes y e Body of
HANNAH WHITE daughter to
Samuel & Hannah White aged 20 years
dec d April y e 8th
1 7 1 8

Here lies buried
The Body of CAPT ALEXANDER SEARS
who departed this life March ye 17th
1 7 5 8
aged 69 years

Here lyes buried the Body of
MRS HANNAH SEARS Widow of
Capt Robert Sears
who departed this life June 25th
1 7 6 9
in the 73^d year of her age

In Memory of
MR EDWARD GRANT
who departed this life June 28th 1 7 9 7
aged 78

" Whee the last trumpet breaths the rending sound
And wakes the sleeping nations under ground
Then shall you in the rank of saints appear
And in your hand a golden scepter bear

Here lyes intered
y^e Body of WILLIAM ROUSE
died January y^e 20th
1 7 0 $\frac{4}{5}$
in y^e 65th year of his age

Here lyes buried
The Body of CAPT SAMUEL HARRIS
aged 53 years who died
March y^e 20th
1 7 4 1

MRS MARY RICHARDS

Here lyes intered y[e] Body of
ARTHUR SMITH
aged about 63 years died May y[e] 17
1 7 0 8

Here lyes y[e] Body of
MRS HANNAH COPP Wife to
Mr Samuel Copp dec[d]
Feb y[e] 2[d] 1 7 2 2

MRS SARAH CLARK
1 7 7 9

In Memory of
MR JONAS CLARK who died Nov[r] 28th
1 7 9 0 aged
64 years 2 months & 17 days

In Memory of
CAPT JOHN PULLING
who departed this life Jan[y] 25th 1 7 8 7
in the 51st year of his age

Here lyes intered the Body of
MRS ELIZABETH SHEFFE Wife to
Mr Will[m] Sheaffe
who departed this life March y[e] 17th
1 7 3 1 $\frac{}{2}$

    *   *   *   *   *

Here lyes y[e] Body of
MRS AMY COPP Wife to
Elder David Copp aged 82 years dec[d]
Nov y[e] 28th 1 7 1 8

Here lyes yᵉ Body of
MARCY MARSHALL yᵉ Wife to
Joseph Marshall
aged 36 years dyed yᵉ 18ᵗʰ of
yᵉ 2 – month 1 7 1 2

Here lyes buried yᵉ
Body of MR JOSEPH BULL
aged 55 years died Feb * *
1 7 4 7

Here lies buried yᵉ Body of
M R J O S H U A A T T W O O D
died August 31ˢᵗ 1 7 7 0
aged 70 years

Here lies yᵉ Body of
DEACON JOHN ATWOOD
aged about 67 years died August 26
1 7 1 4

Here lies yᵉ Body of
ELIZABETH ATWOOD Wife to
Mr Joshua Atwood
died Janʳʸ 15 1768 aged 63 years

In Memory of
MRS REBECCA LITTLEFIELD
Consort of
Capt James Littlefield
who departed this life Sept 17ᵗʰ
1 7 7 3
aged 23 years

In Memory of
MRS ANN CLOUGH Wife of
Mr Samuel Clough
died April ye 2^d 1772 aged 52 years

" My parents gone Greate Heaven O tell me where
Where may I drop my unaffected tear
In fillial gratitude where may I weep
In gratefull silence lull my soul to sleep,
May I awake in heaven & find her there
Where endless raptures qwell each rising care."

Here lies the Body of
MARY GREENWOOD Wife to
Samuel Greenwood
departed this life Sept 21st 1 7 7 4
aged 31 years

In Memory of
MISS NANCY GREENWOOD
daughter of Nathaniel & Pricilla Greenwood
who departed this life May 5th
1 8 0 2
aged 34 years

In Memory of
MR EBENEZER HANCOCK
who died July 4th 1799 in the 50th year
of his age

Here lyes y^e Body of
MRS ABIGAIL BEAL Wife of
Mr Othniel Beal
dec^d Nov y^e 16th 1719 in y^e
25th yeare of her age

Here lyes y[e] Body of
CAPT THOMAS BARNARD
aged 59 years 5 mo & 15 days deces[d]
March y[e] 14th 1 7 1 5 $\frac{15}{16}$

Here lyes y[e] Body of
MR THOMAS BARNARD
aged 46 years dec[d] May the 16
1 7 3 0

WEBSTER.

GRANT WEBSTER died 1797 Æ 80
JOHN WHITE died 1803 Æ 67
SARAH WHITE died 1807 Æ 77

Here lyes y[e] Body of
MRS MARIA ELLIOT Wife to
Capt John Elliot
aged 27 years 11 mo & 8 days dec[d]
Sept y[e] 21st 1 7 2 1

MRS HANNAH NICHOLS
1 7 6 0

This Tomb belongs to the heirs of
MISS ELIZABETH BRONDSON
who departed this life March 20th 1810
Æ 82
GEORGE BRONDSON CURTIS died Aug[t] 20th
1 8 0 0

Here
lies yᵉ Body of
Mᴿ JOHN MILK
decᵈ May 19ᵗʰ
1 7 5 6
aged 47 years 10 m°
& 27 dˢ

Here
lies buried the Body of
MR. WILLIAM BEER
who died
December yᵉ 11ᵗʰ
1 7 5 9
aged 57 years

WILLIAMS.

J O H N W I L L I A M S
Departed this life Sept. 9, 1845, aged
72 years.

"Each lonely scene shall thee restore,
For thee a tear be daily shed ;
Beloved till life can charm no more,
And mourned till pity's self be dead."

Here lies
M R T H O M A S L E E
The Founder of this Tomb who after a long &
usefull Life died on the 16ᵗʰ of July
1 7 6 6
Anno Ætatis 93
Give up his Body to death his Soul to
Immortality
Also
the Body of his Wife
D E B O R A H L E E
daughter of Edward Flint of Salem who
departed this life the 3ᵈ of April
A D 1763
Anno Ætatis 91

Here
lyes buried ye Body of
M^{RS}   D O R C A S   D O U B E L D E
wife to
MR ELIJAH DOUBELDE
who died March 3^d 1739—40 in y^e
39 year of her age

CAPT. S. BRECK.

MARGARET
ye wife of Willia* Snelling aged 46 yeares
deceased the 18 day of Ivne 1667

Here lyes ye Body of
J A M E S   A D A M S
died June 17th 1718 in ye 32 year of his age

Here lyes buried the Body of
NATHANAEL NEWELL JUN^R
aged 26 years 10 m^o & 15 days dec^d April y^e
24th 1 7 1 7

Sacred to the Memory of
MRS HENRETTA HARPER
Wife of the
Rev John Harper late of the Island of St Christophers
who having early in life obtained the faith which
works by love endured as seeing him who is
invisible and rested in peace from all her
labours May 23^d 1795 in the 27th
year of her age

Here lyes yᵉ Body of
Mᴿ PHILLIP HUGHES
aged 62 years decᵈ June yᵉ 16ᵗʰ
1 7 2 9

Here lyes yᵉ Body of
DAVED WEBB ·
died Oct yᵉ 9ᵗʰ 1722
in yᵉ 35ᵗʰ year of his age

Here lies buried the Body of
MRS ESTHER PARKMAN
the virtuous consort of
Mr Alexander Parkman aged 42 years
who died Janʳʸ yᵉ 12ᵗʰ
1 7 4 $\frac{5}{6}$

Here lyes buried the Body of
M R S   M A R T H A   E M M E S
aged 22 years & 9 mᵒ & 6 ᵈˢ
died Janʳʸ yᵉ 27ᵗʰ
1 7 4 $\frac{6}{7}$

Here lyes yᵉ Body of
MRS ELIZABETH TYLEY
wife to Mr John Tyley
decᵈ Sept yᵉ 1ˢᵗ 1727 aged
near 37 years

Here lyes buried
the Body of MR ALEXANDER PARKMAN
died March yᵉ 16ᵗʰ
1 7 4 $\frac{7}{8}$
in the 49ᵗʰ year of his age

Here lyes y^e Body of
SARAH SWAEN Wife to
Benjamin Swaen & daughter to William
& Elizabeth Parkman aged near
97 years
died Feb^{ry} 10th 1710$_{11}$

Here lyes buried y^e Body of
MRS MARTHA DIXWELL Wife to
Mr John Dixwell
who died Oct y^e 3^d
1 7 2 2

Here lyes buried y^e Body of
MRS MARY DIXWELL Wife to
Mr John Dixwell
aged 35 years dec^d Sept y^e 28th
1 7 2 1

Here lyes intered the Body of
MRS LOVE RAWLINS Widow of
Capt John Rawlins
who departed this life December 10th Anno Dom
1 7 4 3
in the 66th year of her age

Here lyes the Body of
MR SAMUEL PARKMAN
who departed this life April the 10th
1 7 6 7

Here lyes buried the
Body of JAMES TOWNSEND
dec^d April 18th 1738
in ye 70th year of his age

Here
lyes the Body of
MR WILLIAM PARKMAN
aged 72 years
dec^d Nouember 28th
1 7 3 0

CHARLES JARVIS
Died Nov. 15, 1807, aged 59 years.
A Physician, a Statesman, a Patriot, and an honest
Man, whose dignified Deportment, sublime Elo-
quence, unbounded Philanthropy, and other
Virtues endeared his Memory to his
Fellow Citizens.

Here lies the Body of
WIL^M BOWES PARKMAN
Son to Mr Samuel and Mrs Dorcas Parkman
died Novr 22^d
1 7 5 8
in the 24th year of his age

---

* * * * * s Buried
* * e Body of
DOROTHY PARKMAN
dau^r to Mr Elias & Mrs Elizabeth Parkman
aged 15 years & 2 m^o dec^d
April ye 9th 1 7 4 1

Here lyes ye Body of
MRS ELIZABETH BELCHER
widow to
Mr Joseph Belcher who departed this life
Aug 23th 1 7 6 2

Here lies buried the Body of
LIEU^{NT} WILLIAM MERCHANT
who departed this life August
ye 12th 1751
aged 61 years

[MASONIC EMBLEMS.]
In Memory of
CAP^T ROBERT NEWMAN
who died March 23^d 1806
Æt 51

Though Neptunes waves & Boreas blasts
Have tost me to and fro
Now well escaped from all their rage
I^m anchored here below
Safely I ride in triumph here
With many of our fleet
Till signals call to weigh again
Our Admiral Christ to meet
O may all those I'v left behind
Be washed in Jesus' blood
And when they leave this world of sin
Be ever with the Lord

Also
In Memory of
CAP^T ROBERT NEWMAN Junr
who died at sea Dec 14 1816
Ætat 31

Here lyes buried y^e Body of
MRS MARTHA SARTLY aged
64 years who died
Feb^{ry} 3^d 1 7 4 7 $\frac{7}{8}$

Here lies y^e Body of
MRS SARAH SHARP
died June 9th 1756 in the 78th year of her age

Here lies buried
the Body of COLO LEONARD JARVIS
who departed this life
the 30th day of September
1 7 7 0
aged 56 years

JOSHUA ELLIS,
Born in Sandwich, May 4, 1769, died July 29,
1 8 2 9 .

SARAH ELLIS,
Born in Lynn, March 3, 1769, died April 2,
1 8 2 3 .

LYDIA L. ELLIS,
Born in Boston, Aug. 13, 1798, died April 2,
1 7 9 9 .

JOSHUA ELLIS, Jun.,
Born in Boston, Nov. 4, 1796, died June 7,
1 8 2 0 .

EMELINE C. D. JOSSELYN,
Born in Boston, Sept. 2, 1833, died Oct. 28,
1 8 3 3 .

J. CULLEN AYRE, M. D.,
Died Jan. 22, 1846, aged 34 years and 4 mos.
Christus Resurrectio et Vita est.

ANTOINETTE D. AYRES,
Aug. 28, 1839, aged 3 years & 7 mos.

EMELINE A. AYRE
Died Jan. 21, 1842, aged 2 months.

HENRY D. EMERSON,
Born in Boston, April 19, 1836, died Aug. 16,
1 8 4 0 .

Like a bright flower he was cut down.

Here lies buried the Body of
MRS ELIZABETH JARVIS Widow of
Capt Nathaniel Jarvis died February 13th
1 7 6 0

Here lies buried the Body of
MARY JONES
the wife of Mr Josiah Jones aged 62 years
died ye 7th * * * 1746

Here lyes buried the Body of
* APT JOSIAH JONES
dec^d Jan^{ry} ye 17th 1744 in the 51st
year of his age

Here lies the Body of
T H O M A S   J O N S O N
dec^d Decr ye 31st 1722 in ye 28th year of his age

Here lies ye Body of
MRS MARCY WHITE Wife of
Mr James White
died April 13th 1778 aged 32 years
" The sweet remembrance of the just " shall flourish when
they sleep in dust.

In Memory of
ROBERT L. TILDEN,
Son of Charles & Isabella Tilden,
who died Nov. 6th, 1801,
aged
2 years & 4 months.
" Sleep on sweet babe and take your rest ;
God call^d you home, & saw it best."

Here lies intered the Body of
CAPT PATRICK CONNEL
who was born in the countey of Kelcaney in
Ireland who departed this life
June the 11th 1763
aged
50 years
Also is buried here 4 of his children

Here lyeth ye Body of
MR THOMAS KELLON
aged 32 years died Dec ye 25th 1708

To the Memory of
BENJAMIN EUSTIS,
who departed this life
May 4th, 1804,
aged 84.

Here lyes ye Body of
JANE
wife to Onesimus dyed April ye 24th
1727
in ye 32^d year of her age
WILL^M
son to Onesimus & Jane aged 10 days
dyed April ye 28th
1727

Here lyes the Body of
MARY FORIST
wife to Charles Forist dec^d Sep^t 2^d
1728
aged 33 years

Here lyes y[e] Body of
MARTHA KNOX dau[r] of Mr Adam Knox
aged 2 years & 7 m[o] died May 15th
1 7 4 8

In
Memory of
MRS ELEANOR READ
departed this life Sept 17th 1798
aged 58 years
MRS ELEANOR GERE
departed this life Sept 19th 1798 aged
30 years
MISS ELIZABETH BERRY
departed this life Sept 21st 1798 aged
25 years
" Depart my friends, dry up your tears,
We must lie here till Christ appears."

Here lyes the Body of
MRS MARY PULLEN Wife to
Mr John Pullen
aged 66 years dec[d] Jan[y] 15th
1 7 3 5

ROBERT KING
son of Mr Henry & Mrs Sarah King
aged 3 months died Sept 19th
1 7 4 *

---

* RASMUS
son to Erasmus & Persis Stevens
aged 2 years dec[d] Nov y[e] 1st
1 7 2 1

Here lies buried
the Body of MRS ANN MALCOM
widow of Capt Daniel Malcom
died April 4th 1770
aged 40 years

Here lyes intered
ye Body of ARTHUR SMITH
aged about 63 years died May ye 17th
1 7 0 8

ELIZABETH VIAL
daughter of John & Mary Vial aged 9 weeks
dyed Ianuary ye 17
1 6 8 2

In Memory of
MRS ELIZABETH COLEMAN
who died Sept 1798
Æ 58
Also
MISS TEMPERANCE COLEMAN
who died Sept 13th 1798
Æ 32

In Memory of
DEACON JOSIAH WILLARD,
died Aug. 20th, 1807,
aged 57 years.

LYDIA WAIR
ye wife of Daniel Wair died Ianuary ye 2d
1 7 0 4 $\frac{}{5}$
in ye 43d year of her age

To the Memory of
WILLIAM FRANCIS,
Son of Mr. Asa Francis, of Hartford, Connecticut,
who died June 26, A. D.,
1 8 0 4 ,
aged 20 years.
" Like flowery fields youth blooming stands,
Pleased with the morning light ;
The flowers beneath the mowers' hands
Lie withering ere 'tis night."

Here lyes ye Body of
MARY HUMPHRES
died October ye 30th 1721 in ye 36th year
of her age

Here lyes ye Body of
MR JAMES SHIRLEY
son of
Mr John & Mrs Jenet Shirley
who died August ye 2^d
1 7 4 9
in ye 31st year of his age

Here lyes the Body of
DEACON EDWARD ALLIN
died Sept ye 29th
1 7 3 9
in ye 30th year of his age

Here lyes the Body of
MRS THEODOCIA HAY
aged 65 years died May ye 31st
1 7 5 5

Here lyes ye Body of
MRS ABIGAIL GOFFE
wife of Mr William Goffe
died August 21st 1744
in ye 49th year of her age

Here lyes buried the Body of
MRS MARY HOLMES
wife to Mr Nathaniel Holmes
Aged 34 years
died July ye 16th 1742

Here lyes ye Body of
MR GEORGE INGERSULL
aged 78 years and three months died August 10th
1 7 2 1

Here lyes buried the Body of
THOMAS GOODWELL
aged 62 years who died
Decr 21st 1749

Here lyes ye Body of
MRS ELIZABETH LIDSTON
who departed this life Febry 6
1 7 5 2
aged 52 years

Here lyes ye Body of
MRS ELIZABETH LAMSON
wife to Mr Nathaniel Lamson
who died August the 10th 1766 aged
33 years

Sacred to the Memory of
MRS LUCY PARRY
wife of Mr Richard Parry who departed this life
Sept 23^d 1800
in the 40th year of her age
Also her son
C O R N E L I U S   C O O K
died Nov 2^d 1791

"Remember the great teacher — death."

Here lies ye Body of
MRS ABIGAIL LOW Wife of
Mr John Low
aged 32 years & 4 mo dec^d
August ye 21st
1 7 38

In Memory of	Also
MR JOHN WILLISTON	MRS ANN WILLISTON
who departed this life	wife of Mr John Williston
7th April	who departed this life
1776	28 Septr 1775
aged 56	aged 52 years

Here lies buried
ye Body of MR JOSEPH GRONARD Junr
aged 22 years & one month
died Nov 19th 1746

Here lies buried the Body of
MR ALEXANDER CAMPBELL
who departed this life August 4th 1770
aged 55 years

Sacred
to the Memory of
MRS LUCY POMROY
wife of
Mr Daniel Pomroy
who died Jany 1st 1805
aged 23 years

VERNON & BROWN'S TOMB.

Here lyes the Body of
FORTESQUE VERNON
who departed this life
Dec 21 1778 Ætat 63
Also
THOMAS C VERNON
who departed this life
Nov 3 1809 Ætat 60

Here lies ye Body of
MRS MARY HUNT
wife of
Mr Daniel Hunt who departed this life
Oct 25th 1801 aged
66 years
" The joys of faith triumphant rise,
" And wing the soul above the skies."

Here lies buried
the Body of MR JOSEPH GILLANDER
of Aberdeen in Scotland died the
31st May 1774

```
┌─────────────────────┐
│   L. RIDGWAY'S      │
│   TOMB. 1819.       │
└─────────────────────┘
```

In Memory of
MR THOMAS ROBBINS
who died March 11th, 1803, in the
49th year of his age.

* * * Let us follow his flight,
" And mount with his spirit above ;
Escaped to the mansions of light,
And lodged in the Eden of love."

```
┌─────────────────────┐
│  SILAS ATKINS'      │
│     TOMB.           │
└─────────────────────┘
```

Sacred to the Memory of
M R S   B E T S E Y   P I T M A N
wife to Mr Joseph Pitman
who departed this life March 8th
1 7 8 4
aged 27 years

" Haste ! haste ! he lies in wait.   He watches at the door.
Insidious Death !   Should his strong hand arrest,
No composition sets the prisoner free.
Death's terror is the mountain faith removes.
" 'Tis faith disarms destruction.
Believe, and taste the pleasures of a God !
Believe, and look with triumph on the grave."

```
┌─────────────────────┐
│     E D E S .       │
└─────────────────────┘
```

JOHN MAVERICK.

J O H N
Son to John and Elizabeth Maverick
aged about 4 years dec^d
Jany 24th 1719

Here lyes buried the Body of
MR RICHARD HENCHMAN
aged 70 years
dec^d February y^e 15th
1 7 2 4 $\frac{}{5}$

In Memory of
MR JAMES CARTER SINGLETON
who departed this life Novr 26th
1 8 0 0
aged 34 years
Depart my friends, dry up your tears ;
I must lie here till Christ appears.

In Memory of
CAPT BEJ^N HAMMATT
who died Apr 7th
1 8 0 5
Ætat 93

Here lyes y^e Body of
MRS ELIZABETH BARNARD
wife to Capt Thomas Barnard aged about
58 years dec^d September
ye 14th 1716

MR. JOHN BRIGGS.

Sacred
To the Memory of
MR. NICHOLAS BROWN,
who died May 14,
1 8 0 1 ,
Aged
40 years.

Sacred
To the Memory of
MRS. ELIZABETH BROWN,
Wife of
Mr. Nicholas Brown,
who died Dec. 11, 1803.
Aged 35 years.

When the last scene — the closing hour — drew nigh,
And earth receded from her swooning eye,
Tranquil, she left this transitory scene,
With decent triumph, and a look serene ;
By faith she fixed her ardent hopes on high,
In Jesus' merits, and in him did die.
So shall her grave with rising flowers be drest,
And the green turf lie lightly on her breast.
Here shall the morn her earliest tears bestow,
'Here the first roses of the year shall blow,
While angels with their silver wings o'ershade
The ground now sacred by her relics made.
Then rest in peace beneath this sculptured stone,
Till Jesus' trumpet calls thee to his throne.

Sacred to the Memory of
M R .   J O H N   B A N K A M P ,
who died March 21st
1 8 0 5 ,   aged 34 years.
He was a native of Prussia, on his return from the
West Indies to his native country. It may
with truth be said of this worthy stranger, that in his life, he was an example of * * odness & great-
ness of mind rarely to
* e met with, and
died the
DEATH OF THE RIGHTEOUS MAN.

MR. WILLIAM CLOUGH.
1 7 8 9

Here lies buried the Body of
MRS HANNAH TUTTLE
wife to Mr Elisha Tuttle dec^d
May ye 15th 1736
in ye 67 year of her age

Here lyes buried
the Body of CAP^T THOMAS TEMPLER
who was born in the city of Exeter and
died August ye 3^d
1 7 4 5
aged 47 years

Here lyes ye Body of
MR DAVID CRAWFORD
born in Greenock in Scotland, who dec^d
Novr 20th 1738
a g e d 5 4 y e a r s

In Memory of
MRS MARGARET
wife of Mr John Boies of Waltham and daughter of
Mr Robert Duncan, died Oct 21st
1779 Æ 60

Here lyes buried
the Body of MRS MARY BLACKADOR
widow of Capt Christopher Blackador
aged 43 years died Oct 23^d
1 7 5 1

Here lies deposited
The Remains of HEZEKIAH WYMAN,
Son of William & Elizabeth Wyman,
who died Oct. 24, 1808,
Æ. 6 years & 5 mo.

" Fresh in the morn, the summer rose
   Hangs withering ere 'tis noon ;
   We scarce enjoy the balmy gift,
   But mourn the pleasure gone.
   Should this assuage our keenest pain,
   Our loss is his eternal gain."

Here lyes ye Body of
CAPT JOHN SUNDERLAND
aged 64 years deceased
September ye 11th
1 7 2 4

Here lyes ye Body of
MR THOMAS LASINBY
who died June 24th A D 1747 aged
60 years

Sacred to the Memory of
M R   P E T E R   G I L M A N
who departed this life April 12th 1807
aged 42 years

" Stop my friends, and in a mirror see
  What you, though e'er so healthy, soon must be.
  Beauty, with all her rosebuds, paints each face ;
  Approaching death will strip you of each grace."

Here lyes ye Body of
MRS SARAH BROWN Relict of
Mr James Brown late of Ipswich dec^d departed
this life May 16th 1772
Aged 76

This Monument, erected June 4, 1848, by
ROBERT G. SHAW,
Son of FRANCIS SHAW JR., and HANNAH NICHELS,
as a tribute of Respect to their Memory.

MAJOR SAMUEL SHAW,
third son of Francis and Sarah, served as an officer in
THE REVOLUTIONARY WAR,
from its commencement to its close.
On the 22d of February, 1784, he sailed from
New York in the ship Empress of China, for
Canton, as supercargo and part owner.
This being the first vessel that
sailed from the United States
for that place, he was
appointed by
WASHINGTON, Consul to China,
which office he held until his death, in 1794.

In
Memory of
F R A N C I S   S H A W ,
born in Boston,
1 7 2 1 ,
died October 18, 1784,
aged 64.

S A R A H   B U R T ,
his wife, born in Boston, 1726, died
September, 1799,
aged 74.
Their children were

FRANCIS JR.,
died at Gouldboro', Maine, 1785,
aged 37.

JOHN,
died at Gouldboro', Maine, 1780,
aged 30.

SAMUEL,
died on his passage from Canton, 1794,
aged 39.

WILLIAM,
died while on a journey at Charlemont, 1803,
aged 46.

ABIGAIL,
wife of John Crocker,
died at Washington, D. C. August 12, 1797,
aged 49.

NATHANIEL,
died on his passage from Canton,
1791,
aged 30.

JOHN BURT
died January 7, 1745, aged 54.

WILLIAM BURT
died February, 1752, aged 26.

SUSANNAH BURT
died February, 1752, aged 21.

SAMUEL BURT
died September, 1754, aged 30.

ABIGAIL BURT
died August, 1778, aged 90.

BENJ. BURT
died 1803, aged 75.

NATH. HOWLAND
died July, 1766, aged 62, and ABIGAIL, his wife,
died 1766, aged 49.

Here lyes ye Body of
MR TIMOTHY THORNTON
aged 79 years
dec^d Sep^t ye 19th
1 7 2 6

Here lyes ye Body of
M^{RS} SARAH THORNTON
wife of Mr Timothy Thornton aged 86 years
dec^d Decr ye 3^d
1 7 2 5

ELIZABETH LORING
dau^r to Mr David & Mrs Elizabeth Loring
died Sep^t 23^d 1767
aged 17 months

Here lies buried the Body of
MRS ABIGAIL ADAMS Wife of
Mr Benjamin Adams who departed this life
Jan^{ry} the 17th 1764
in the 35th year of her age
& EUNICE her babe 7 weeks old

Here lyes buried the Body of
CAP^T JOHN DOBEL
died the 8th of April 1773 aged 70 years

Here lies buried
the Body of MRS ABIGAIL DOBEL
wife to Captain John Dobel
who departed this life November the 5th
1 7 6 9
aged 59 years

In Memory of
MRS MARY DOBEL
who died Decr 3^d 1790 Æt 55
also her husband
CAPT JOSEPH DOBEL Senr
died March 19
1 8 1 0 Æt 71
"Here rest the dead, from sin and sorrow free,
They are gone to heaven, O God, we trust to thee,
Their bright examples may we make our own,
As far in Christ as they themselves were known."

Here lyes y^e Body of
MR THOMAS HUNT aged 73 years &
7 months who dec^d Feb^{ry} y^e 11th
1 7 2 1 $_2$

Here lies buried
the Body of **MRS SARAH BUTLER**
wife to Mr Joseph Butler
died October 25th 1754 aged 38 years
& 7 months

JACOB HEWINS
aged 36 years dec^d July y^e 6 1690

JACOB HEWENS
son of Jacob & Martha Hewins
aged 4 days died Oct y^e 7
1 6 7 3

Here lyeth y^e Body of
NICHOLAS STONE aged 76 years
died December ye 9
1 6 8 9

JEAN TREUIS
LATE WIFE TO
DANIELL TREUIS
AGED NEAR
❚00 YEARS
DIED JUNE Y^E 30
❚706 ^{7}

NOTE. — This stone is but ten inches high, eight wide, and six thick. It stands fifty feet east of Dr. Jarvis's monument.

In Memory of
MR BENJAMIN GOODWIN
died Nov 30th 1792
aged 61 years
MRS HANNAH GOODWIN
died Oct 25th 1775
aged 42 years wife to Mr Benjamin Goodwin
NANCY WEATHERSTON GOODWIN
died Oct 21st 1775 aged 11 days
daughter of
Mr Benjamin & Mrs Hannah Goodwin

Here lies the Body of
MRS SARAH BENNETT Widdow of
Capt Ellis Bennett who departed
this life July 31st
1765
in the 68th year of her age

In Memory of
MR ELIJAH SWIFT
who died May 9th 1803 aged 73 years
" A wit's a feather, and a chief's a rod;
An honest man's the noblest work of God."

In Memory of
MRS EDEE SWIFT Wife of
Mr Elijah Swift who died
Oct 12th 1795
aged 64 years

Here lyeth buried y^e Body of
LYDIA GARISH
y^e wife of John Garish aged about 27 years
dec^d January y^e 8th
1 6 2 $\frac{7}{8}$

Here lyeth y^e Body of
LYDIA WATTS
aged 55 years dec^d September 29
1 7 0 0

ELIZABETH TOUT	MARY
aged 42 years	TOUT
dec^d Oct y^e 24	AGED 1
1 6 7 8	YEAR
SARAH TOUT	DYED
aged 5 weeks	OCTOBER
died	Y^E 19
1 6 7 8	1 6 7 8

WILLIAM ELLIS
son to William & Susannah Ellis
aged 2 year & 7 m^o died
Sep^t y^e 8th
1 6 9 4

ELLIS
son to Mr Ellis & Mrs Mary Bennet deceased
July y^e 23^d 1733

GOD

Ephesians 1, 9.      1 John iv. 8.

1 Cor. xv. 49.   Matthew v. 9.

Is Love.

Erected by

ISAAC DUPEE,

Grandson to G.

Aged LXXV.

August, 1846.

" My name from the palms of his hands
Eternity will not erase ;
Impressed on his heart, it remains
In marks of indelible grace.
Yes, I to the end shall endure,
As sure as the earnest is given,
More happy, but not more secure,
The glorified spirits in heaven."

SUSANNA BARR
wife to John Barr aged 40 years died
March y^e 6 170$\frac{1}{2}$

Here lyes buried y^e Body of
JAMES INGLES
aged 70 years & 6 mo deceased
Febuary y^e 6
1 7 0 $\frac{2}{3}$

Here lies y^e Body of
MRS MARTHA TUCKS
aged 65 years dec^d y^e 4th November
1 7 2 9

Here lyes y^e Body of
MRS MARY PERKINS
y^e wife of Capt William Perkins
she died July 8th
1 7 5 6
aged 38 years

Here lyes y^e Body of
MRS SARAH SARVISE
the Wife of Mr Samuel Sarvise dec^d Augst 4th 1739
in the 30th year of her age

Here lyes ye Body of
MR GEORGE SHARROW
aged 54 years
who died Oct 6th 1743
also
HEMMEN HENDERSON
aged 18 years died April 19th
1 7 3 8

Sacred to the Memory of
CAPT. RALPH BEATLY,
who departed this life
October 16th,
1 8 0 4 ,
aged 42 years.
" While holy friendship drops the pious tear,
    And mournful garlands deck the hallowed bier,
Can bounteous heaven a greater solace give
Than that which whispers, ' Friends departed, live.' "

In Memory of
CAPT JOHN BUCKLEY
who died on Fryday 9th August 1799
aged 58 years

MR. JOHN MORRISON.

MRS. NANCY DOMACK.

In Memory of
MRS NANCY HOLDEN the Wife of
Mr Thomas Holden
who died 25th May 1802
aged 19 years 2 months & 4 days
also an infant buried with her

In Memory of
ENOCH HOPKINS
who departed this life Decr 27 1778
Æ 55 years
" Tell them tho' 'tis an awful thing to die,
    'Twas e'en to thee ; yet the path once trod,
Heaven lifts its everlasting portals high,
And bids the pure in heart behold their God."

Here lies the Body of
M R   S A M U E L   J O N E S
dec^d Augt y^e 26
1 7 3 1
in y^e 42^d year of his age

Here lyeth buried y^e Body of
JOHN IRELAND
aged 18 years & 7 months & 10 days
died February y^e 15
$1\,7\,0\,\frac{1}{2}$

Here lyes y^e Body of
MARY HILL Wife to Edward Hill
aged about 42 years
did Jany 20th
$1\,7\,2\,1\,\frac{1}{2}$

EDMUND HARTT'S
TOMB. 1806.

Here lyes y^e Body of
MRS LYDIA CULLAM Wife to
Capt John Cullam who died
Nov y^e 3^d 1761 aged
42 years

Here lies y^e Body of
MRS MARY NOWEL Wife to
Mr Thomas Nowel
aged 45 years dec^d May y^e 29th
1 7 3 9

In Memory of
MRS HANNAH GILES, Wife of
Mr. John Giles, who died
August 12, 1805, aged 26 years.
A native of Plymouth, England. Also, her
infant son.

" Surviving friends, dry up the falling tear,
A little while our Saviour will appear ;
Prepare to meet with joy at Christ's right hand,
Where, free from sin, each saint will perfect stand."

Here lyes buried ye Body of
ROBERT SEARES
who departed this life December 29
1 7 3 2
in ye 76th year of his age

Here lyeth buried ye Body of
ABIGAIL BILL
wife to Thomas Bill aged 63 years
died
November ye 7th
1 6 9 6

Here lies buried
the Body of CAP^T JOHN DORRINGTON
Obit 14th March 1772
Ætatis 44

Here lyes ye Body of
MRS ANN WALDO Wife to
Mr John Waldo aged about 31 years
died Feb^ry 2^d
1 7 2 3
also a child still born

SARAH ROUS
Wife to William Rous died August 29
1 7 0 5

Underneath this monumental stone
lies deposited
The Body of MR. JOSEPH HEMMINGWAY,
who departed this life Jany 15th,
1 8 0 6 ,
aged 59 years.
He was a respectable man and worthy citizen
to his country.

" My children, do not mourn,
Nor drop one tear when I am gone ;
Where I am gone I am at rest,
Pray think me numbered with the just."

Here lies ye Body of
SAMUEL HOPKINS Son to
Mr Enoch & Mrs Mary Hopkins who died
Sep^t 23^d 1767
aged 1 year & 8 months

In Memory of
MRS PRISCILLA SNELLING
widow of Joseph Snelling who departed this life
August 2^d 1791 aged 79 years

In Memory of
MRS. ELIZA FULLER,
Wife of Mr. John Fuller, who died
Sept. 16th, 1806, aged
22 years.

" An angel's arm can't snatch me from the grave,
Legions of angels can't confine me there."

In Memory of
MRS REBECCA SNELLING
who departed this life May 26th 1802
in the 63 year of her age

---

* O H N
son to Thomas and Silence Barnard
aged 16 mo and 28 days died Sept ye 5th
1 7 1 9

In Memory of
MRS HANNAH BROWN,
widow of the late Bartholomew Brown,
obt. March 29th, 1810, aged
50 years.

" Mother and friend, our heavy loss is thy eternal gain ;
Thou 'rt run thy race, hast borne thy cross, and art released
from pain.
May we, whom thou hast left below, like thee fulfil our part,
Like thee when Jesus bids us go, be ready to depart."

Here resteth the Body of
JOHN BUCKLEY Junior, Son of
John Buckley of Saddleworth, Old England,
Merchant, who departed this life the
23^d day of August,
1 7 9 8 ,
in the 23^d year of his age.

" In peace here rests a traveller's dust,
His journey 's at an end ;
He prized esteem among the just,
A censure from a friend.

" Broke loose from time's tenacious charms,
And earth's revolving gloom,
To range at large in vast domains
Of radiant worlds to come."

MARY RIND	WILLIAM RIND
Age * * *	aged about 1 year dyed
died ye 15 of August	ye 14 of February
1 6 6 2	1 6 6 6

NOTE. — This is the oldest monument. It was dug up some years ago by Mr. Glidden.

Here lyes ye Body of
ELIZABETH KING Wife to
John King aged about
38 years died Nov y^e 20th
1 7 1 5

This Stone is in Memory of
MRS ELIZABETH McKEAN
Wife to Mr William McKean
who died 8th of July 1792 in the 44th year
of her age

Here lies y^e Body of
MRS DORCAS PHILLIPS
Wife to Mr Anderson Phillips who died
June y^e 9th 1767$_{\overline{8}}$ * * * * *

---

* * * * * es buried * * e Body of
MRS HANNAH NICHOLS
wife to Mr William Nichols dec^d March 22^d
1 7 6 9
aged 56 years

In Memory of
MARY CREIGHTON dau of George &
Mary Creighton died April 5th
1 8 0 1
Æ 2 years & 7 mo

Sacred to the Memory of
MR. ELIJAH CORLEW,
who departed this life May 25th, 1804, aged
31 years ;
also, his infant child.

" Lo, soft remembrance, drops a precious tear,
And holy friendship stands a mourner here."

Here lyes y[e] Body of
MRS DORCAS PEGGY
wife to Mr Edwad Peggy aged 65 years
died October the 24
1 7 2 0

Here lyes y[e] Body of
ELIZ[H] ADAMS daut to Joseph & Eliz[th]
Adams aged 30 years & 6 m[o] dec[d]
Nov y[e] 2[d] 1725

Here lyes y[e] Body of
RICHARD FURBUR Son of
Mr Richard & Mrs Abigail Furbur who died
March 8th 1749
aged 6 years & 8 months

Here lies buried the Body of
MR RICHARD FURBUR died Feb[ry] 15th
1 7 5 3
aged 38 years

Here lyes buried the Body of
MR JONATHAN MASTERS
aged 44 years dec[d] Feb[ry] y[e] 12
1 7 3 2

Here lyes y^e body of
MR ISAAC ADAMS aged 59 years
who died December 30th * * *

---

* ere lyes y^e Body of
* ANNAH CARTHEW aged 66 years
dec^d Jany 20th 17$\frac{13}{14}$

Here lyes intered the Body of
MR LEONARD DROWNE who departed
this life Oct y^e 31st 1729 in y^e 83^d
year of his age

Here	Here
lyes the Body of	lyes the Body of
MR PHILLIP MERRITT	MRS MARY MERRITT
dec^d March y^e 29th	wife to
1 7 4 1	Mr Phillip Merritt dec^d
in y^e 70th year of	Sept y^e 20th 1735 in
his age	y^e 60th year of her age

Here lyeth y^e Body of
J A M E S   B A R T E R
aged 71 years died May 16 1757

Here lyeth buried y^e Body of
MATHEW PITTOM y^e son of
John & Mary Pittom aged near 20 years
died January y^e 26th 1 6 9 $\frac{3}{4}$

Here lyeth buried y^e Body of
MOSES DRAPER
aged about 31 years dec^d y^e 14th August
1   6   9   3

Beneath this stone are deposited
The Remains of MRS. MARY LEWIS,
Widow of Capt. Winslow Lewis, who departed
this life December 31st, 1806,
aged 60 years.

This Monument is erected
In Memory of MRS. SARAH MULVANA,
who died July 4, 1805, aged
68 years.

"Farewell, my friends, dry up your tears ;
I must lie here till Christ appears."

Sacred to the Memory of
MRS. BETHIA GILMAN,
Wife of Peter Gilman,
who departed this life Jany 22^d, 1806,
aged 40 years.

Here lyes the Body of
SALLY GOODWIN Wife to
Capt Charles Goodwin of Charlestown &
eldest daughter of Mr John & Mrs Sarah Strong
of Newburyport who departed this life
Augt 23^d 1781 aged
25 years

" My hope is fixed, my spirit's free,
Longing my Saviour for to see ;
Such joy and bliss doth fill my soul,
Nothing on earth doth me control.
My loving husband and infant small,
My parents dear, I leave you all.
My soul doth wing the heavenly way,
My Saviour's call I must obey.
Read this and weep, but not for me,
Who willing was to part with thee,
That I may rest with Christ above,
In peace and joy, and endless love."

In Memory of
MRS LYDIA GILMAN Wife of
Mr Peter Gilman
who died March 6th 1796
in the 28th year of her age
"She's gone, and with the righteous mounts on high,
With joy and everlasting ecstacy."

In Memory of
MRS. ABIGAIL GILMAN, Wife of
Mr. Peter Gilman,
who died July 3[d], 1802, aged
29 years.

Sacred to the Memory of
PETER GILMAN JR., Son of
Peter and Lydia Gilman, who died July 11th,
1 8 0 4 .

In Memory of
ELIZA LANE PROCTER,
daughter of Mr. Benjamin and Mrs. Eliza Procter,
who died Oct[r] 15th,
1 8 0 2 ,
aged 1 year and 6 months.

Here lies buried the Body of
MR JOHN WHITE ROBERTS
died Nov 20th 1771
aged 36 years

BENJAMIN LARRABEE
son of Deacon William & Mrs Lydia Larrabee
dec[d] May 9th 1730 aged 3 years &
10 months

In Memory of
MRS MERCY ROBERTS Relict of
Mr John White Roberts
who died May 2^d
1 7 9 9
aged 61 years

" The joys of faith triumphant rise,
And wing the soul above the sky."

Here lyes ye Body of
MRS JANE CHAMBERLIN
Relict of Mr John Chamberlin who died
May 20th 1738
aged 68 years

> WILLIAM DODD'S
> TOMB. 1807.

Here lyeth buried ye Body of
WILLIAM WATERS
ye son of Samson & Rebecca Waters
aged 21 years 3 mo & 12 days

Sacred to the Memory of
MISS POLLEY TOWNSEND
who died March 9th
1 7 8 7
aged 9 years & 5 months
also
Judith Ebenr John James R & Benj B Townsend
children of
Mr Nathan & Mrs Judith Townsend

Here lyes ye Body of
ELIZTH STRETTON dau^r of
William & Elizth Stretton aged 33 years
9 mo & 26 days dec^d Feby 15
1 7 2 0 21

Here lyes buried the Body of
MRS ELIZABETH SARGEANT
wife to Mr Thomas Sargeant
who departed this life May the 19th 1770
aged 60 years

Here lyes ye Body of
MRS DORCAS DEMOUNT Wife to
Mr John Demount
who died May 19th 1738
aged 55 years

Here lyes ye Body of
MARY ADAMS
Wife to Nathaniel Adams aged 77 years
died June ye 11th
1 7 0 7

Here lyeth buried ye Body of
KATHRON WAY
ye wife Richard Way aged about 55 years
who deceased ye 28 day of Aprill
1 6 8 9

Here lyes ye Body of
MRS SARAH MILLER Wife of
Mr James Miller
aged 45 years died Feb^{ry} 6th
1 7 5 5

JANE
daughter of Joseph & Mercy Burdsell
aged 1 year & 8 mo died
1 7 2 1

Underneath this turf
rests the Sacred Remains of
MR. CALEB BEAL, who died
Dec. 10th, 1801, Ætat.
55 years.

Here lyes ye Body of
MRS ELIZABETH BURRINGTON
wife to Mr Thomas Burrington
died June ye 2d
1 7 2 3
in the 24th year of her age

Here lyeth ye Body of
GRACE GAMMAN aged 74 years
decd July ye 27
1 7 0 2

In
Memory of
JUDITH TOWNSEND died Oct 16th
1 7 7 1
aged 3 days
Nathan Townsend died * * * 16th 1777
aged 10 months
John Townsend died June 27th 1783
aged 2 years & 7 months
the children of
Mr Nathan & Mrs Judith Townsend

Here lies buried
The Body of Master ROBERT PATRIDGE,
Son of Robert and Mary Patridge,
who departed this life,
Nov. 10th, 1802,
aged 14 years, 1 month, and 27 days.

" Sleep on, dear youth, and take thy rest." * * *

In Memory of
MR BENJAMIN POOL
who died Oct 5th 1795 aged 65 years also
In Memory of
MRS ANN POOL
wife of Mr Benjn Pool

MOSES BASS'S TOMB.
1819.

Here lyes the Body of
MRS ANN WINDSOR Wife to
Mr Thomas Windsor
who died Nov 25th 1745 aged 57 years

SARAH ELLIS
aged 70 years deceased on ye 4th day of September
1 6 8 1

Here lies ye Body of
REBECA TWING aged 36 years
died Jany ye 5th
1717 18

Memento
Mori Fugit Hora
Here lyes yᵉ Body of
FURNELL SMALLPIECE
Son of John & Olive aged 6 years & 4 mo
died August 28ᵗʰ
1 7 1 2

Here lyeth yᵉ Body of
LEFT MATHEW BARNARD
aged 54 decᵈ yᵉ 9ᵗʰday of May
1 6 7 9
Also
his mother **ALCE BARNARD**
died 1663 & Mary Barnard his last child dyed
1 6 6 3

Here lyeth intered
yᵉ Body of **THOMAS KEMBLE**
aged 67 yeares & 14 dayes
decᵈ January yᵉ 29
1 6 8 8

Here lyes yᵉ Body of
WILLIAM LOWD Son of
John & Dabrah Lowd aged 28 years
deceased yᵉ 17 of December
1 6 9 0

Here lyeth intered yᵉ Body of
MAIOR ANTHONY HAYWOOD
aged about 50 years departed
this life yᵉ 16 of October
1 6 8 9

Here lyes ye Body of
MRS MARGARET THATCHER
Wife to Mr Thomas Thatcher
aged 38 years died Sept ye 14
1 7 1 9

In Memory of
MR CLEMENT COLLINS
who departed this life
April the 24th
1 7 8 7

Here lies ye Boddy of
MRS JERUSHA CADDALL
wife of Mr Robert Caddall died Novr 14th
1 7 7 1
in ye 30th year of her age
" O cruel Death, that would not to us spare
A loveing wife, a kind companion dear ;
Great it is to friends that 's left behind,
But she, we hope, eternal joys did find."

Here lyes the Body of
MRS MARY GYLES wife to
Mr Charles Gyles died Oct 30th 1757
in the 59th year of her age

Here lies buried the Body of
CAPT PHILLIP BREADING
who departed this life November 22^d
1 7 6 4 aged 63 years

Here lies ye Body of
PELATIAH KINSMAN
aged 47 dec^d April ye 2^d 1797

Here lyes buried the Body of
MRS ABIGAIL TAYLOR departed this life
Oct 26th 1774 aged 75 years
& 9 months

Here lyes buried the Body of
JONATHAN ADAMS
aged about 64 years died April ye 7th
1 7 0 7

Here
lyes buried ye Body of
MR ROBERT CUMBY
aged 62 years & 5 months
decd July 17th 1717

Here lyes buried
the Body of MRS REBECCA CUMBY
wife to Mr Robert Cumby
deceased April ye 26
1 7 3 1

Here lyes buried the Body of
MRS SARAH MALCOM Wife to
Mr Michael Malcom died
Sept 23d 1767

In Memory of
MARY WATERS,
Wife of Capt. Daniel Waters ; formerly wife of
Mr. Peter Mortimore, born in the city of
Waterford, in the kingdom of Ireland.
She died June 7th, 1802,
Æt. 78.

Here lies ye Body of
ANN RUBY
dau^t of John & Elizath Ruby aged 17 years
died Sept ye 19th
1 7 4 1

In Memory of
J O H N   K E N T
son of Seth & Elizath Kent who died
30th Sept 1794 aged
6 years

| GEORGE SUTHERLAND'S |
| TOMB. 1809. |

Here lies buried
the Body of **MRS CHARITY COLLINS**
wife to Deacon Joseph Collins
who departed this life
Oct 25th 1741
in the 67th year of her age

Here lyes ye Body of
MRS PATIENCE COLLINS
wife of Deacon Joseph Collins who suddenly
departed this life June the 25th
1 7 6 0
aged 67 years

Here lyes ye Body of
MRS MARY GARDNER
wife of Mr John Gardner aged 39 years dec^d
ye 22^d May 174*

In Memory of
B E T S E Y ,
Wife of David Darling, died
March 23ᵈ, 1809,
Æ. 43.
She was the mother of 17 children, and around
her lies 12 of them, and two were lost at sea.
BROTHER SEXTONS,
Please to leave a clear berth for me
near by this stone.

Here
lyes the Body of
CAPT JOHN HOBBY
aged about 50 years died Sept yᵉ 7
1 7 1 1

CAPT.
PETER MORTMER.

Here lyes yᵉ Body of
MRS SARAH BASS yᵉ widdow of
Capt Phillip Bass died April yᵉ 26
1 7 4 6
in yᵉ 86 year of her age

A SAMUEL returned to God in Christ
After a short abode on earth
To avoid earth's harmes and crimes
Was here well put to bed betimes
The graveˢ as short as thou prepare
Lest thy death come at unaware

NOTE. — This is an ancient monument, without date, fifteen
feet east of the Winslow Tomb.

Tomb No. 59.

JONATHAN MOUNTFORT.

1 7 2 4 .

Tomb No. 7.

MR. JOHN MOUNTFORT,

ÆTATIS LIV. OBT.

JAN. VI.

MDCCXXIV.

BENJAMIN MOUNTFORT

SON OF

JOHN MOUNTFORT AND MARY MOUNTFORT,

ÆTATIS XXV.

OBT. MARCH X. MDCCXXI.

Sacred to the Memory of
MR. EBENEZER PARSONS,
who died August 31, 1805,
aged 23 years.

Here lyes intered
the Body of MR JAMES MORTIMER
who departed this life August 18th
1 7 7 3
aged 69 years
He was born in the city of Waterford in the
kingdom of Ireland

Here lyes intered the Body of
MRS HANNAH MORTIMER
who departed this life August 21st
1 7 7 3
aged 81 years
She was born in the city of Waterford
kingdom of Ireland

Here lies buried
the Body of CAPT EDWARD PAGE
who died July 27th 1785
aged 34 years

Sacred to the Memory of
MR. SAMUEL WELLS,
who resigned this life Nov. 13th,
1 8 0 4 ,
in the 26 year of his age.

"Stop, my friends ; in a mirror see
What you who ere so healthy be,
Tho' beauty with her rosebuds paint each face,
Approaching death will strip you of each grace."

JOSEPH FARNUM
aged about 30 years dec^d Nove^r ye 30
1 6 7 8

U * tima semper expe * * anda dies hom * * e diciquc beatus
Ante obitum nemo supremaque funera debit

Here lyes buried the Body of
M R D A N I E L G R A V E S
of the island of Barbados
aged 32 years died
July ye 10
1 7 3 9

Here lyeth buried ye Body of
JOHN GILL
aged about 60 years dec^d ye 10 day of December
1 6 7 1

Here lyeth buried ye Body of
ELIZABETH
wife to John Gill aged about 35 years
dec^d ye 28 of Sept^r
1 6 6 6

Vive Memor Lofthy Memeinto Mori.
Sacred to the Memory of
MR. GEORGE TOMPKINS,
who died Octr 21st,
1 8 0 1,
Ætat. 25.

" Beneath this humble stone here lies a youth
Whose soul was goodness, and whose heart was truth;
Crop't like a flower he withered in his bloom,
Though flattering life had promised years to come."

Here lyeth buried the Body of
SARAH GRANT
relict of Edward Grant aged about 61 years
dec^d y^e 25 of March
1 6 9 0

Here lyes y^e body of
SAMUEL
Son to Obadiah & Elizabeth Gill
aged 3 years & $\frac{1}{2}$
departed this life y^e 29 of
May 1 6 8 3

Here lies the Body of
MRS ABIGAIL CADES Wife of
Mr John Cades died Sept 3^d
1 7 7 7
aged 37 years

Here lyes the Body of
MR JOHN DETHICK
aged 68 years dec^d
July y^e 2^d 1738

Here lyes y^e Body of
MRS ANN HOBBY
Wife of William Hobby
aged 74 years died
Iune ye 22^d
1 7 0 9

Here lies ye Body of
ROBERT EDMUNDS
aged 89 years dec^d Nov y^e 22^d
1 7 1 7

Here lyes buried the Body of
MRS SUSAN BENTLY Wife to
Mr Thomas Bently aged
42 years who died
Sept y^e 9th
1 7 4 8

Here lyes buried
the Body of MRS SARAH BREED
the wife of
Mr Nathaniel Breed aged 54 years & 10 months
dec^d March 5th 1739$\frac{4}{40}$

Here lyes buried y^e Body of
MR JOSIAH BAKER
who died June y^e 19th 1729 in y^e 74th
year of his age

SARAH BALLARD
y^e wife of Daniel Ballard aged 46 years
died December y^e 15th in y^e year
1 7 0 4

Here lyes y^e Body of
MRS DORCAS PHILLIPS
Wife to Mr Anderson Phillips who died
Jany 9th 1763 aged
* * * *

Here lyes ye Body of
MR DAVID EDWARDS
son of Mr David & Mrs Mary Edwards
aged 43 years & 4 mo dec^d Dec ye 4th
1 7 2 7

Here lies the Body of
MR JOHN BATTENS Jun[r]
late of St Johns Newfoundland who departed
this life April 1st
1 7 6 2

Here lyes y[e] Body of
MRS MEHETEBLE PRATT
Wife to Mr William Pratt
who departed this life August 8th 1750
in the * * * * year
of her age

Here lies buried the Body of
MRS ABIGAIL SHERBURN
Wife to Dea[n] Thomas Sherburn departed
this life April 8th
1 7 7 8
aged 61 yeares

SARAH WINSLOW
aged 26 yeares died y[e] 4 day of April
1 6 6 7

Here lyes buried y[e] Body of
MRS LYDIA WHITEMORE Wife to
Mr John Whitemore J[r] died
Jan 5th 1750 aged
31 years

In Memory of
MRS MARTHA BROWN
who died
Sept 20th 1795 aged 78 years

ELIZABETH
daughter of Thomas & Elizabeth Barnard
aged 2 years dyed y° 4 of Sept
1 6 8 3

ELIZABETH
daughter of Joseph & Lydia Williams
aged 1 year & 8 mo
died August y° 12
1 6 9 0

Here lyes intered the Body of
HENDRIETH HIRSST
aged about 52 years deceased January y° 30th
1 7 1 7

In Memory of
M I S S   E L I Z A ,
eldest daughter of Mr. William Mills and
Mrs. Betsey, his wife, died
August 20th, 1809,
Æ. 17 years and 6 mos.

In Memory of
MR. SAMUEL WAKEFIELD,
who died Nov. 12,
1 8 0 9 ,
Æ. 22.

" This humble stone proclaims the truth —
Here lies a much respected youth,
But now cut down in early prime,
And far beyond the ills of time.
In brighter worlds and clearer skyes
Shall all his manly virtues rise."

Here lyes yᵉ Body of
MRS AMMEY HUNT
wife of Mr Benjamin Hunt who died
Nov 20th 1769 aged
40 years

"A sister of Sarah Lucas lieth here,
Whom I did love most dear;
And now her soul hath took its flight,
And bid her spightful foes good night."

Here lies buried the Body of
MRS SARAH HUNT
who departed this life Dec 26 1775 aged
99 years

" Blessed are the dead who die in the Lord, for they rest from
their labors."

WILLIAM BOYNTON
and
JOHN E. LOW'S
Family Tomb.

Here lyes buried the Body of
MRS MARY PAYSON
who died June 3d
1 7 4 3
in the 36th year of her age

Here lies buried the Body of
MR JOSEPH BEATH
who died July 28th 1780 aged 26 years

Here lyes yᵉ Body of
HANNAH HOBBY yᵉ Wife of
John Hobby
aged about 27 yeares decᵈ June 26 169 *

Here lyes yᵉ Body of
M R S   M A R Y   H U G H E S
dauʳ of Mr Richard & Mrs Sarah Hughes
who died March yᵉ 7 1765
aged 46 years

" Time, what an empty vapor 'tis,
And days, how swift they fley !
Our life is ever on the wing,
And death is ever nigh.
The moment when our lives begin,
We all begin to die."

Here lyeth buried
yᵉ Body of
SUSANNA SWEET
yᵉ wife of
John Sweet
aged 44 years deceased
yᵉ 16 of July
1 6 6 6

Here lyeth buried
yᵉ Body of
JOHN SWEET
aged 82 years
departed
this life yᵉ 25 of
April
1 6 8 5

Here lyeth buried yᵉ Body of
DANIEL GEORGE
aged 29 years deceased yᵉ 18 day of July
1 6 8 4

Here lies yᵉ Body of
MR ABRAHAM GORDUNG
aged about 76 years died Sept yᵉ 27
1 7 0 6

Here lyeth buried ye Body of
D A N I E L   T R A V I S   S e n i o r
aged 76 years departed this life
ye 19 of January 1688₉

Here lyes ye Body of
MRS WILLMOUTH HOAR
aged 78 years dec^d Feb^ry ye 29th
1 7 3 5 ₆

> JAMES W. BURDETT.
> 1809.

Here lyes ye Body of
J A M E S   G O D M E R
aged about 39 years deceased July ye 12th
1 7 1 5

* * es buried * * e Body of
M R S   H A N N A H   N I C H O L S
dec^d March 22^d 1769
aged 56 years

Here lyes buried the Body of
MRS MARY ELA
who dec^d March ye 6th 1737₈ in y^e
55 year of her age

Here lyes ye Body of
MRS MARY SUMERS Wife to
Mr Edward Sumers aged 72 years dec^d
Novr ye 18th 1724

Here lies buried the Body of
MR WILLIAM GODNER
who departed this life Sept 12th 1769
aged 60 years

Here lies buried the Body of
CAPT PHILLIP BASS
who departed this life June 10th
1 7 6 1

THOMAS FRACKER
and
COTTON THAYERS.

Here lyes the Body of
MR RICHARD TREW
died October 8 175*
in the 26 year of his age

Here lyes buried the Body of
MR JOHN GOFFE
decd July ye 24th 1716 in the 67th year
of his age

Here lyes buried ye Body of
MRS ELIZABETH SNELLING
who died April ye 1st A D
1 7 3 7
aged 32 years 11 mo & 14 ds

Here lies ye Body of
MR RICHARD LACK
died Feb 29th 1760
Æ 86

Here lies the Body of
MRS MARY OWEN Wife of
Mr William Owen
who departed this life December ye 14th
1 7 6 7
aged 66 years

Here lyes ye Body of
R I C H A R D   R A N D A L L
who dec^d October ye 10th
1 7 3 0
aged 38 years

Here lies the Body of
MRS HANNAH EDMONDS
wife of Mr Joseph Edmonds who died
suddenly Sept 19th 1778
aged 45 years

Here lyes intered the Body of
MRS ANN ARCHER
wife to Capt Thomas Archer who died
Sept 20th 1738 in ye 69th
year of her age

Here lyes ye Body of
S * M U E L   K N I G H T
aged 32 years died
October 25th
1 7 2 1

Here lyes buried the Body of
WILLIAM BROWN died Sept ye 6th
1751 aged 54 years

Here lyes y[e] Body of
MRS MARY RUSSELL
who died Sept y[e] 29th
1 7 5 0
aged * * * * *

Here lyes buried the Body of
MOSES PAULL
son to Mr Moses & Mrs Mary Paull
aged 27 years 2 months & 25 days dec[d] March
y[e] 25th 1730

Here lyes buried
the Body of MRS ELIZABETH WISWALL
wife to Mr Peleg Wiswall dec[d]
Dec[r] y[e] 1st 1743

Here lies buried the Body of
MR FRANCIS MARSHALL
who departed this life the 24th
of July 1767 aged 57
years

Here lyes buried y[e] Body of
MR JOHN BROWN
who died suddenly March y[e] 11th
1 7 4 7 $\frac{}{8}$
aged 45 years & 8 mo

THOMAS GATTE
son to Capt Pattrick Gatte & Rachel his wife
aged 5 years & 2 mo
died Dec[r] 7
1 7 4 5

Here lyes y^e Body of
MRS CHARITY BROWN
consort to Mr John Brown who departed
this life April y^e 13
A D 1 7 5 4
in y^e 31st year of her age

SAMUEL WHITEHEAD
son of Samuel & Mary Whitehead aged 1 year
6 months & 22 dayes
dec^d August 26th 1719

Here lyes buried the Body of
M R S A M U E L B R O W N
who died Aug 7th 1786
aged 57 years

Here lyes buried the Body of
NATHANIEL NEWEL
aged 73 years dec^d Nov ye 29 1731

Here lies intered the remains of
GEORGE EUSTIS
Son of Mr Benjn Eustis who departed this life
Oct 19th 1779
in the 25th year of his age

Here lyes y^e Body of
M R S R E B E C A B L A C K M A N
wife to y^e Reu^d Mr Benjamin Blackman aged
about 63 years dec^d
March y^e 20th 1715

MRS LYDIA GENDALL

Capt * ELEG L HILMAN
1 7 9 8

___

Here
lyeth y^c Body of
CAPT DAVID EDWARDS
aged about 57 years died October y^e first
1 6 9 6

___

Here lyes y^e Body of
MR DANIEL TUCKER
dec^d July 17th 1739
in y^e 32^d year of his age

___

Here lyeth buried
y^e body of JOHN SOAMES Senr
aged about 52 years departed
this life November y^e 16
1 7 0 0

___

Here lyeth y^e Body of
HINDRETH HURST aged about 52 years
departed this life Nouember y^e 16
1 7 0 0

___

Here
lyes y^e Body of
MRS ABIGAIL BEALE
wife of Mr Othniel Beal dec^d Nov y^e 16th
1 7 1 9
in y^e 25th year of her age

In Memory of
LUCY SWIER who died
Oct 1 1795 * * * * * *

O

that they were wise, that they would consider their latter end.

* ere lies buried
the Body of MRS HANNAH COLLINS
wife to Mr Daniel Collins who died
May 8th 1756
in the 42 year of her age

MRS SARAH COLLINS
1 7 7 1

R Y

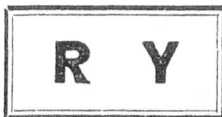

NOTE. — This stone has no date. It stands thirty feet west of the chapel.

In Memory of
MR ENOCH HOPKINS
who departed this life Dec 27 1778
Æ 55 years

Here lyes ye Body of
S A R A H   S H E R R I N
wife to Richard Sherrin
aged 46 years & 4 months decd Aug ye 26th
1 7 1 5

Here lyes buried
ye body of Richard Sherrin aged 52 years
departed this life October ye 22d
1 7 1 0

Here lyeth buried the body of
SAMUEL WINSLOW
aged 39 years departed this life
October ye 14
1 6 8 0

Here lies buried the Body of
M R S   H A N N A H   P A R K M A N
wife to Mr William Parkman
died May 14th 1756
aged 62 years & 5 months

SARAH IAMSON
aged about 83 years died ye 23th daye of March
1 6 9 6

Here lies ye Body of
D A V I D   N O R T O N
aged 57 years Decmbr 2^d
1 7 2 1

Here lyes ye Body of
M A R Y   T H O M A S
dau^r to Mr John & Mrs Lydia Thomas
of Brantry dec^d Sep^t ye 4th
1 7 3 4
in ye 20th year of her age

Here lyes buried ye body of
JUDITH HUNT
ye wife of Thomas Hunt aged about 38 years
departed this life ye 18 of October
1 6 9 3
A daughter of Capt William Torrey of
Waymouth.

Here lyes the Body of
MR JOHN PARKER
who died Sept 27th 1744 in ye 80th
year of his age

Here lyes ye Body of
MRS SARAH PARKER
wife of Mr John Parker died Sept 5th
1 7 5 0
in ye 81st year of her age

S A R A H
G R E E N O V G H
A G E D 5 D Y E D
S E P T E M B E R
1 6 7 6

Here lies buried the Body of
MRS HANNAH HARRIS
widow of Capt Leach Harris
who died Dec 24th 1783 aged 67 years

"The memory of the just
Shall flourish when they sleep in dust."

Here lies buried the Body of
MR JOHN HARRIS
died Decemr 18th 1770 aged 68 years

Here
lies buried the Body of
MRS PRUDENCE NEWELL
wife of Mr John Newell died Febry 21st
1 7 7 7
in the 36th year of her age

In Memory of
MRS SALLY DUMBLIDE
who departed this life Feb^ry 26th 1796
aged 35 years

Here lies buried the Body of
NATHANIEL HARRIS
son of Mr John & Mrs Anna Harris
aged 20 years died Feb^ry ye 12
1 7 4 9

Here lies intered the mortal part of
MR EDWARD PAGE
who departed this life November the 10th
1 7 8 4 aged 68 years

Here lyes ye Body of
S A M U E L B A B C O C K
died Oct ye 24th 1721 in ye 31st year
of his age

Here lyes ye Body of
SUSANNAH DOUBLEDAY
dau^r of Capt John & Mrs Eliz^th Doubleday
died Sept 5th 1773 aged 20 months

Sacred to the Memory of
M R S . A N N S I N G L E T O N,
who died Sept. 3^d,
1 8 0 5,
aged 29 years.

" Happy soul, thy days are ended,
All thy mourning days below ;
Go, by angel guards attended,
To the sight of Jesus go."

Here lies buried the Body of
MR JOHN CARTER
who died Nov 26 1765 aged 65 years
Also
MRS JANE CARTER
wife to Mr John Carter who died July 28th
1 7 7 2
aged 57 years

"In Death's cold arms our bodys lays
Until we hear the sound ;
Then shall we rise, our God to praise,
And leave the meaner ground."

GEORGE SINGLETON
departed this life Jan. 24th, 1805,
Æt. 39.

In Memory of
JAMES CARTER SINGLETON,
who departed this life Nov. 26th, 1800,
aged 34 years.

"Depart my friends, dry up your tears,
I must lie here till Christ appears."

Here lyes buried ye Body of
MRS MARY HILL
aged about 55 years died the 20 of Oct
1 7 1 4

Here lyes buried ye
body of Capt William King died June 20th 1 7 6 8
aged 43 years
Also
WILLIAM KING
son to Capt William & Mrs Mary King
died April 7th 1767

Here lyes ye Body of
JOHN BARBER Sen^l
aged 84 years dec^d December ye 4th
1 7 2 6

Here lyes ye Body of
JOHN TILESTON
dec^d Oct ye 7th 1721 in ye 16th year of
his age

Here lies the Body of
MR JOSIAH KING
who departed this life
* * * * * * * * *

Here lies intered the Body of
COL WILLIAM BURBECK
died July 22^d 1785 aged 69 years

Here lies buried the Body of
MRS JERUSHA BURBECK
wife of Col William Burbeck
died July 27th 1777 aged
54 years

Here lyes y^e Body of
CAPT DAVID ROBERTSON
aged 63 years died July 3^d
1 7 2 6

Here lyes y^e body of
MARTHA SHUTT
wife to William Shutt aged 51 years died
Jan^ry y^e 8th 1721$\frac{}{22}$

HERE LYES THE MORTAL PART OF
WILLIAM CLARK ESQ.,
AN EMINENT MERCHANT OF THIS TOWN, AND
HONORABLE COUNCILLOR FOR
THE PROVINCE,
Who distinguished himself as a faithful and affectionate
Friend, a fair and generous Trader,
LOYAL TO HIS PRINCE,
yet always zealous for the Freedom of his
Country, a Despiser of
SORRY PERSONS
and little Actions, an enemy of Priestcraft and
Enthusiasm, a Lover of good Men of
various Denominations, and a
reverent Worshipper
of the DEITY.

Reliquæ
JOHANNIS CLARKE Armig

laudatissimi senatoris et medicinæ doctoris

probitate modestia

et mansuetudine præclari

terram reliquit Decem 5 1728 ætat 62

Nomen et pietas manent post funera

Note. — This monument is twelve feet west of south front gate.

Sacred to the Memory of
MISS MERCY JONES,

who died April 7,

1 8 0 5,

aged 20 years and 6 months.

" Adieu, my friends, forever, ever gone,
Her happy soul has put full glory on ;
The tenderest ties could never her detain,
But O, our loss is her most happy gain.
Gentle her manners were, her taste refined,
Her face an emblem of her heavenly mind ;
Her speech sincere, and open as her heart,
Her conversation did delight impart.
Though young, she listened to the voice of truth,
And trod a Savior's steps in early youth ;
Calm and serene, she yielded up her breath,
And even triumphed at the approach of death."

Here lies buried ye Body of
MRS SARAH GOOLD

wife to Capt James Goold died Oct 11th 1764

aged 73 years

NOTE. — The following lines are on an old monument, without name or date.

" What is 't fond mortal y^t thou wouldst obtain
     By spining out a painful life of cares ;
Thou livest to act thy childhood o're again,
     And nought intends but grief and seeing years.
Who leaves this world like me, just in my prime,
Speeds all my business in a * * * * time."

Here lies buried the Body of
MR RICHARD SHERRIN
aged 53 years died Dec y^e 25
1 7 4 6

In Memory of
MARY ARMSTRONG
dau^r of Mary Huntley who departed this life
Sept 28th A_D 1798 in the 36th
year of her age

In Memory of
MARY HUNTLEY
who departed this life Sept 28 1798
in the
64th year of her age

" Stop here, my friend, & cast an eye,
     As you are now, so once was I ;
     As I am now, so you must be,
     Prepare for death & follow me."

MARY PERKINS
dau^r of Isaac & Mary Perkins aged
11 years 3 mo & 28 days dec^d
July ye 3^d 1718

Here lyeth buried y[e] Body of
JOHN WHITE
aged about 50 years dec[d] y[e] 6 of August
1 6 2 5
NOTE. — The true date of this inscription was 1695. It was altered some forty years ago by a school boy.

Here lyeth buried y[e] body of
CAPT WILLIAM GREENOUGH
aged about 52 years dec[d]
August y[e] 6th
1 6 9 3

Here lies the Body of
MRS ELIZABETH STONE
wife of M[r] William Stone who departed
this life March y[e] 15th
1 7 6 3
in the 57th year of her age

JOSEPH
son to Joseph & Hannah Calley
aged about 7 years dec[d]
Nov[r] y[e] 28th 1678

Here lyes y[e] Body of
SARAH
y[e] daughter of William & Sarah Clark
aged 18 months died August y[e] 15
1 7 0 4

Here lyes y[e] body of
MRS ELIZABETH FORSYTH
wife to Capt Alexander Forsyth died July y[e] 28th
1726 in y[e] 30th year of her age

To the Memory of
MARTHA,
daughter William & Nancy Grubb, who
departed this life Sept. 21st,
1 8 0 5 ,
aged 1 year & 16 days.
"Sweet babe, thou art gone to Christ thy friend,
Who takes sweet children in his arms,
And there to sleep till time shall end,
Secure from sorrow or alarms."

In Memory of
MRS. SARAH HUNT,
wife of Mr. Joab Hunt, who departed this life
May 18th, 1805, aged
65 years.

In Memory of
MR. JOAB HUNT,
who departed this life March 14th,
1 8 0 0 ,
aged 62 years.

---

* * * * * * * * * WARD
OBiit June 22d 1790 Ætat 56
Also
CATHARINE
his wife OBiit Jany 3d 1801 Ætat 64
Also
JAMES SEWARD
grandson of James & Catharine Seward
OBiit Sept 22d 1792
Ætat 6 months
He bore a lingering sickness with patience, and
met the king of terrors with a smile.

Here lyes buried yᵉ Body of
ANNA HENCHMAN
wife to Nathaniel Henchman aged 37 years
& 9 mo died Janʸ 7ᵗʰ 1706

GRANT
Family Tomb.

ELIZABETH GRANT	died	May	25,	1769,	Æt. 20.
MOSES GRANT	"	August	18,	1777,	Æt. 70.
ELIZABETH GRANT	"	Jan.	28,	1778,	Æt. 70.
SAMUEL GRANT	"	Nov.	14,	1784,	Æt. 79.
SARAH GRANT	"	March	14,	1792,	Æt. 39.
MARY GRANT	"	Dec.	3,	1808,	Æt. 27.
MOSES GRANT	"	Dec.	22,	1817,	Æt. 73.
JOHN GRANT,	"	Sept.	19,	1820,	Æt. 33.
ANN GRANT	"	April	17,	1832,	Æt. 77.
SUSAN W. GRANT,	"	July	26,	1818,	Æt. 31.

Here lyes yᵉ Body of
M A R Y ,
yᵉ wife of Ceasor Augustus servant of
Mr Robert Ball aged 25 years
died May 28ᵗʰ 1759

In Memory of
J A M E S G.,
Son of John and Emely Sullivan,
died Febʳʸ 10ᵗʰ, 1807,
Æ. 4 years and 6 mo.

" Why do we mourn departing friends,
Or shake at death's alarms?
'Tis but the voice that Jesus sends,
To call them to his arms."

Here lie the remains of
MR. TIMOTHY GAY,
Merchant, who died July 28, 1719, in the
36th year of his age. He was diligent in his business, faithful
to his friends, and affectionate to his
family.

"Life's little stage is a small eminence, inch high, the grave
above — that home of man where dwells the multitude. We
gaze around, we read their monuments, we sigh ; and while we
sigh, we sink, and are what we deplore."

Sacred to the Memory of
MRS. ANN McMILLIAN,
wife of Mr. James McMillian, who
died Febry 28th, 1805,
aged 81 years.

"Happy soul, thy days are ended,
All thy mourning days below ;
Go, by angel guards attended,
To the sight of Jesus go."

Also,
In Memory of their son,
MR. EDWARD McMILLIAN,
who died at the Island of St. Thomas, W. I.,
Decr 22d, 1804, aged 40.
"He lived beloved, and died lamented."

In Memory of
CHARLES G.,
Son of John and Emily Sullivan, died
Augt 15th, 1815, aged
5 years.
"He's gone to the mansion of rest."

In Memory of
JOHN,
Son of David and Rebecca Adlington, who died
Jany 17th 1816, aged 3 years.
Also,
REBECCA,
aged 1 year, died July 1st
1 8 1 6 .
"Suffer little children to come unto me, for of such is the
kingdom of heaven."

Here lies buried the Body
MRS ELIZABETH TURELL
who died April the 12th
1 7 6 5
in ye 36th year of her age
Also
FOUR of her offspring

Here lyes buried the Body of
MR THOMAS LAWLOR
aged 61 years died Feb^{ry} ye 26th
1 7 4 3 ¼

Here lyes ye Body of
WILLIAM GOODING
aged 17 years died Jan^{ry} 22^d
1 7 3 8 ⅜

In Memory of
MRS. SEETH RUMNEY,
who died suddenly, Jany 13th 1804,
Æt. 56.
The late amiable consort of Capt Edward Rumney.

Here lies the Body of
M R J O S E P H B E A T H
died Jan^{ry} 24th 1771
aged 57 years
Also
MRS SEETH BEATH
widow of Mr Joseph Beath died June 20th
1 7 7 9
aged 66 years

Here lyes ye Body
ISAAC AVES
son of Mr Samuel & Mrs Mary Aves
aged 27 years & 13 d^s dec^d
Sept 24th 1739

Here lyes the Body of
M R J O H N R I C H A R D S
who died Jan^{ry} 5th 1732
aged 29 years

Here lyes buried y^e Body of
M R E D W A R D R I C H A R D S
son to Mr Edward Richards died
February y^e 11th
1 7 4 7 $\frac{}{8}$
aged 70 years
In
Memory of
MR IOSEPH RICHARDS
Son to Mr Edward & Mrs Mary Richards
who died at Port Mahone
January y^e 18th
1 7 4 2
aged 24 years

Here lyes the Body of
ELIZ^H HARRIS
dau^r to Mr Samuel & Mrs Hannah Harris
who dec^d Oct y^e 10th 1744
aged 18 years

Here lyes y^e Body of
MRS MARCY LASENBY
ye wife of Captⁿ Thomas Lasenby
aged 65 years dec^d
August ye 31st
1 7 3 2

Here lyes buried the Body of
M R S   M A R Y   J A R V I S
wife to Mr Elias Jarvis Junr
aged 21 years died
Septr 20th
1 7 4 8

JOHN H. PITMAN'S
TOMB. 1848.

Here lies buried the Body of
M R   P E L E G   W I S W A L L
late Master of the North Grammar School
died Sept 7th 1767 in the
84th year of his age

M A R Y
ye dau^r of Mr James & Mrs Anne Jeffs
aged 4 years 4 mo 12 d^s dec^d
August ye 1st 1734

In Memory of
MRS DEBORAH GARDNER
wife of Capt Lemuel Gardner who departed this life
28th September 1792 aged
39 years
" A loving wife and tender parent."

Here lyes buried the Body of
MR MICHAEL DENNIS
who departed this life
July the 11th
1 7 6 3
in the 48th year of his age

In Memory of
MRS MARY ADAMS
widow of Capt John Adams who departed
this life May 16th 1791
aged 38 years

In Memory of
MR THOMAS CHRISTY
who died Oct 21st 1798
aged 62 years

In Memory of
MRS HANNAH CHRISTY
wife of Mr Thomas Christy who died
Oct 16th 1798

In Memory of
THOMAS CHRISTY
died July 22^d 1762 aged
12 months

JOHN CHRISTY
died Oct 5th 1784 aged 2 years & 9 months

Sacred to the Memory of
MR. JOHN LAMBORD COOPER,
who departed this life Nov. 17th,
1 8 0 5 ,
Æt. 60.

"Hear rests the dead, from pain and sorrow free,
He's gone to heaven, we trust, O God, to thee;
His bright examples may we make our own
So far in Christ as he himself was known."

Here lyes intered the mortal part of
SIMEON SKILLIN
who departed this life February 27 1778
Æ 62 years

Here lyes buried the Body of
M R S   M A R Y   S K I L L I N
wife of Mr John Skillin Junr
died Jan^{ry} 28th 1763
aged 27 years

Here lyes ye Body of
MRS ELIZABETH LASH
wife to Mr Nicholas Lash who died Augst 14
A D 1 7 5 0
in ye 44th year of her age

Here lies intered the mortal part of
RUTH SKILLIN
Relict of Simeon Skillin who departed this life
May 29th 1786 Æ 64 years

Here lyes the Body of
MRS ABIGAIL RICHARDS
dau to Mr Edward & Mrs Mary Richards
died Nov ye 4th 1745 in y[e]
36th year of her age

CHARLES HOLMES.

HENRY LANE.

DANIEL JOHNSON.

TOMB. 1807.

Here lies ye Body of
MRS REBECCA MICHELL
who departed this life Sep 3 1784
aged 59 years

In Memory of
ANNA MILLER
dau[r] of Mr William & Mrs Anna Miller
who died May 7th 1782 aged
12 months

In Memory of
WILLIAM N.,
Son of Ephraim and Nancy Steel, who died
Dec[r] 21st, 1815, aged
3 mo. & 6 days.

"Just like an early rose
We've seen an infant bloom;
But sudden, oft before it blows,
Death lays in the tomb."

In Memory of
S E W A L L ,
Son of Mr. & Mrs. Sally Fisk, who died
April 3ᵈ, 1817, aged
1 year

Here lyes yᵉ Body of
M R S   A N N A   J E F F S
wife to Mr James Jeffs
who decᵈ July yᵉ 22ᵈ 1738 in yᵉ 32ᵈ year
of her age

Here lyes the body of
JONATHAN KENT, A. M.,
who deceased Decembʳ 30ᵗʰ, 1760, aged
43 years.
His Education and temper of mind were liberal.   He
was no Sectary in Religion ; to life or death he
was so indifferent, that, confiding in the divine providence, he was satisfied with
that lot and portion by God for
him ordained in this life
and the future.   Of
himself he might
truly say,
Et inea virtute me involvo probamque pauperiem
sinc Dote quæro.

Here lyes yᵉ Body of
MRS MARY GARDNER
widow of Capt Habakkuk Gardner who departed
this life Decembʳ the 17ᵗʰ
1 7 6 2
aged 56 years

Here lyes yᵉ Body of
MRS JOHANNA LASH
wife to Mr Robert Lash who departed this life
May the 29th 1771 aged 27 years

Here lies buried the Body of
MR THOMAS ADAMS
who departed this life December 31ˢᵗ
1 7 8 1
aged 68 years

Here
lies buried the Body of
MR. RICHARD GOODING
who died suddenly May 16th
1 7 5 6
aged 53 years and 4 months

Here lyes yᵉ Body of
MRS ELIZABETH TUFTON
wife to Capt Thomas Tufton who died Augˢᵗ yᵉ 18th
1 7 6 0
aged 35 years

Here lyes buried the Body of
CAPT BENJAMIN SEWARD
who departed this life February 10
1 7 6 6
in the 29th year of his age

In Memory of
CAPT. EDWARD RUMNEY,
who died April 6, 1808,
Æ. 63.

Here lies buried the Body of
MR JOSEPH BEATH
who died July 28th 1780 aged 26 years

Here lyes ye Body of
MOSES PAUL PAYSON
son of Mr Jonathan & Mrs Mary Payson aged
12 years & 8 mo dyed Janry 20th
1 7 4 2

Here lyes buried the Body of
MRS MARY PAUL
wife of Mr Moses Paul who died May 7
1 7 4 2

Here lyes buried
the Body of MR MOSES PAUL
aged 53 years 3 months who decd Janry ye 5
1 7 3 0

Here lyes ye Body of
SAMUEL MOWER
son of Mr Ephraim & Elizth Mower
died May ye 6th
1 7 4 7

Here lies buried the Body of
MR NATHANIEL BROWN
who departed this life Nov ye 30th
1 7 6 1
in the 48th year of his age

In Memory of
MR JOHN HOSON
who died March 7th 1791 in the 69th year of his age

Here lyes ye Body of
S A M U E L   G Y L E S
son of Mr Edward & Mrs Abigail Gyles
died Octr 25 1773
aged 4 years & 6 months

In Memory of
MRS ELIZABETH LANE
who died April 13th 1795
aged 40 years
A loving wife and tender parent "
Also
AMMI LANE
died 1780 aged 19 years
*   *   *   *   *   *   *   *

died 1743

In Memory
MRS. JOANNA WILLISTON,
wife of Mr. Joseph Williston, who departed this life
Feb^{ry} 23^d, 1803, aged 28 years.
NOTE. — The design on this monument is an urn and weeping
willow.

Here lyes buried
the Body of MRS SARAH TOWNSEND
wife to Mr Thomas Townsend
aged 86 years
died Decr 1st 1750

JOHN DONCAN
son to Mr John & Mrs Keziah Doncan
aged 13 months & 11 d^s dec^d
May ye 29th 1736

Here lies the Body of
MR JOHN ROBERTS
son of Mr Benjamin & Mrs Priscilla Roberts
aged 36 years & 3 mo died Jan^ry 17
1 7 6 5

Sacred to the Memory of
ELIZA ROBERTS
dau^tr of Rich^d & Mercy Roberts, obt. Sept. 12th,
1 8 0 3 ,
Ætat. 13 5 m.

"Poor, weak and worthless though I am,
I have a rich, Almighty Friend;
Jesus, the Savior, is his name,
He freely loved, and without end."

Here lies buried the Body of
MISS ABIGAIL BREADING
who departed this life the 17th day of December
1 7 6 2
aged 13 years & 6 months

In Memory of
MRS ELIZABETH BROWN
wife to Mr Thomas Brown who died July ye 19th
1 7 5 6
aged 37 years
MR THOMAS BROWN
who died March ye 11th 1760 aged
43 years and
ELIZABETH BROWN
dau^r to Thomas & Elizabeth Brown who died
January ye 9th
1 7 6 5
in ye 20th year of her age

WILLIAM
son to
William & Abigail
Merchant
aged 3 years
died Octr ye 16th
1 7 2 1

MARTHA
dau^r to
William & Abigail
Merchant
aged 10 mo & 9 days
died Oct ye 16th
1 7 2 1

In Memory of
T H O M A S L . ,
Son of John & Jane Fisk, died Sept. 24th,
1 8 1 5 ,
aged 4 years.

HANNAH SOAMES
aged 7 months 22 days died ye 30 of
ye 2^d m^o 1674

Here lies ye body of
MRS MARGARY SHARP
wife of Capt Jonathan Sharp died Decem^r 2^d
1 7 6 3
aged 78 years

* * * * es ye Body of
* * * * *ETH KEMBLE
Ag * * * * years
died December 19th
1 7 1 2

MARY PARKMAN
Novr 16th 1763
aged
18 years 3 months &
8 days

SARAH PARKMAN
died June 10th 1765
aged
14 years 1 mo &
5 days

In Memory of
MRS. HANNAH BRIGHAM,
wife of John W. Brigham, who died May 7th,
1 8 0 1 ,
aged 27 years.

In Memory of	In Memory of
RACHEL C. COLE,	ISAAC COLE,
who died Jan. 23,	who died Oct. 20,
1 8 0 0 ,	1 8 0 1 ,
aged 3 mos.	aged 9 mos.

Children of Charles Cole Junr & Rachel his wife.

---

* * re lyes ye Body of
PRISSIELLA WOODDARD
wife to Mr Nath Wooddard dec^d Decr ye 29th
1 7 2 2
in ye 35th year of her age

MR NATHANIEL LEWIS
1 7 7 8

Here lyes buried ye Body of
MR JOHN FOSTER
who departed this life the 12th of Oct^r
Anno D 1746
aged 57 years 8 months & 3 days

In Memory of
MRS HANNAH TILTON,
wife of Mr. William Tilton, who died Nov. 11,
1818, Æt. 38.
" Blessed are the dead which die in the Lord."

Here lyes the Body of
MRS ELIZABETH SCARLET
wife to Mr Humphrey Scarlet dec^d June ye 26th
1 7 3 3
in ye 43^d year of her age

HANNAH NEWHALL
wife to Mr Henry Newhall, departed this life
April 29th 1785 aged 71 years
" O cruel Death, that would not to me spare
A loving wife, a kind companion dear ;
She now her Savior's beauty does behold,
And joins to sing his praise on harps of gold."

Here lies the Body of
MR HENRY NEWHALL
died March 30th 1753 in ye 58th year of his age

JOHN NICHOLL
son of Mr James & Mrs Eunice Nicholl
aged 20 months
died Sept ye 11th
1 7 4 7

Here lyes ye Body of
MRS MARY BENNET
wife to Mr John Bennet aged about 29 years
dec^d March ye 28th
1 7 2 8

In Memory of	In Memory of
MR. ALEXANDER	MRS. MARY
BAKER,	BAKER,
who died May 22^d,	who died Decr 27th,
1 8 0 1,	1 8 0 1,
aged 72 years.	aged 59 years.

Here lyes buried the Body of
MR JOSIAH BAKER
who departed this life April ye 12th
1 7 6 0
in ye 70th year of his age

Erected in Memory of
M R . P H I L L I P   R O S E ,
who departed this life March 20th, 1800,
aged 27 years.

Here lyes ye Body of
MRS ELIZABETH BAKER
wife to Mr Josiah Baker who died June 10th
1 7 5 3 aged 65 years

Here lies buried the Body of
M R S   D O R C A S   T Y L E R
wife of Mr Elisha Tyler who departed this life
Decem^{br} the 28th 1770
Ætat 29

Here lyes the body of
MRS MARY PAGE
wife to Mr John Page aged 29 years
died April 6th 1750

In Memory of
MR. JOHN CREASE,
who died Decr 8th, 1800, in the 33^d year
of his age.

"How loved, how valued once, avails thee not,
To whom related, or by whom begot ;
A heap of dust alone remains of thee,
'Tis all thou art, and all the proud shall be."

Sacred to the Memory of
MR. SAMUEL LORD,
who died
July 29, 1808, Æ. 56.

Died, Nov. 5th, 1804,
MRS. ELIZA MARIA REVERE,
Æt. 28, a Native of the City of New York, wife of
Mr. Edward Revere, of Boston, Silversmith.

" Death with his dart hath pierced my heart,
While I was in my prime ;
When this you see, grieve not for me,
'Twas God's appointed time."

ISABELL RICHARDSON	ANNE RICHARDSON
died July 20th 1730 aged	died July 22 1730 aged
1 year & 2 mo	2 years & 2 mo

& children of
Mr Richard & Mrs ****** Richardson

MRS CATHERINE RICHARDSON
1 7 9 2

Here lies intered the Body of
ANDREW ELIOT, D. D.,
Pastor of the New North Church,
who died
Sept. 13th, 1778,
Ætat. 66.

JOHN,
Son of John & Lydia Gunderson, died
Novr 12, 1817, Ætat.
7 years.

MARTYN.

Here lies y^e Body of
E D W A R D   P A G E
son of Mr Edward & Mrs Rebeckah Page
aged 5 years died Septr y^e 8th
1 7 6 0

Here lies the Body of
M R S   A B I E   S A L T E R
widow of M * * * * Salter * * * * * *
* * * years * * *

Here lyes ye Body of
MRS ELIZABETH STEPHENS
wife to Mr John Stephens aged 38 years dec^d
Novr 19th 1725

Around this monumental Stone
lies intered the Remains of eight children of
Saml & Mary Lord
SAM^L LORD Junr aged 8 years
POLLY LORD aged 1 month
POLLY LORD aged 10 years
SAMUEL LORD the Second aged 4 years
HARRIOT LORD aged 1 year
THOMAS LORD aged * * * *

Here lyes ye Body of
M R   T H O M A S   S C O O T
who died Sept ye 3^d
1 7 3 3
aged about 50 years
Also
Here lyes ye Body of
M R S   A N N A   S C O O T
wife to Mr Thomas Scoot who died May ye 6th
1 7 3 4
aged 59 years & 6 mo

In Memory of
T H O M A S   B A R R Y,
who was drowned in Boston Harbor,
Aug. 30, 1807,
aged
21 years

In
Memory of
MRS. PATIENCE S. STEVENS,
who died Dec. 23^d, 1814,
Ætat. 37.

MARY LEMMER
died Jany 18th, aged 11 years and 6 months

In Memory of	In Memory of
MR DAVID	MRS ELIZABETH
PULSIFER	PULSIFER
who died Sept 26th 1797	wife of David Pulsifer
in the	who died Dec 2^d 1807
56th year of his age	in the 61st year of her age

This Stone is erected in Memory of
MRS. DEBORAH BLAKE,
wife of Mr. William Blake, obt. the 3^d of August,
1 7 9 1 ,
aged 21 years & 7 months.

" Friend, as you pass, suppress the falling tear ;
You wish her out of heaven to wish her here."

Here	Here lyes * * body of
lyes ye Body of	MRS MARGRET BOMMOR
MR THOMAS BOMMOR	wife of
aged 74 years	Mr Thomas Bommor
dec^d June 1st	aged 72 years dec^d
1 7 4 1	Feby 22^d 1741

In Memory of
MISS REBECCA PERKINS,
dauh^r of Mr. James & Mrs Sally Perkins,
who died March 16, 1802,
aged
19 years, 7 months, & 13 days

" My friends and parents, do not mourn,
Nor drop one tear now I am gone ;
Where I am gone I am at rest,
Pray think me numbered with the blest."

MARINERS' TOMB.

This Tomb is Dedicated to
SEAMEN OF ALL NATIONS,
BY
PHINEAS STOW,
Pastor of the First Baptist Bethel Church, Boston,
1851.

" The dead shall be raised."

Deposited in the
Mariners' Receiving Tomb,
E M I L Y ,
Wife of Rev. Phineas Stow, of Boston,
who suddenly departed this life
May 18, 1851, aged
42 years.
The tribute of respect
paid to the departed by seamen
and friends is very consoling to the bereaved
husband and his motherless daughter.
Her devotion to the welfare of
mariners gave her the appropriate appellation of
THE SAILOR'S FRIEND.
Her excellent judgment made her a safe adviser in
temporal and spiritual things. Cheerfulness
and frankness were prominent features
in her character. Monuments more
durable than marble or brass
are erected to her mem-
ory in loving
hearts.

"She rests from her labors."

" Her sun went down while it was yet day."

No parting kiss, no dying words to cheer,
But years of love, enshrined in memory dear,
Shall wake devotion on affection's shrine,
While musing on thy life and theme divine.

"Not lost, but gone before."

The remains of these four Seamen have also been deposited in the Mariners' Tomb.

HANS PETER JOHNSON,
Born in Sweden,
Died in Boston,
March 20th 1851,
aged 30 years.

HENRY SHAPLEY,
Died April 23, 1851,
aged 45 years.

FRANCIS JAMES,
Died April 22^{d} 1851.
aged 28 years.

ALONZO THAYER,
Died June 2^{d} 1851,
aged 39 years.

Sacred to the Memory of
MR ELIJAH ADAMS
who departed this life Augst 25 1798
in the 61st year of his age

"O Death, thou hast conquered me,
I by thy dart am slain;
But Christ will conquer thee,
And I shall rise again."

Sacred to the Memory of
MISS POLLY TOWNSEND
who died March 9th
1 7 8 7
aged 9 years 3 months
Also
Judith Eben^r John James R & Benjn B Townsend
children of Mr Nathan & Mrs Judith Townsend

In Memory of
M R   B E N J A M I N   P O O L
who died Octr 5th 1795
aged 65 years.
Also
In Memory of
MRS ANNA POOL
wife of Mr Benjamin Pool

Here lies buried the Body of
MRS MARY WHITE
wife of Mr Benjamin White
died Feby 23^d
1 7 5 9

Here lies ye Body of
M R S   H A N N A H   W I N D S O R
wife to Mr Thomas Windsor
who died Novr ye 25 1745
aged 59 years

Here lyeth ye Body of
A B I G A I L   H A N Y F O R D
wife of John Hanyford
aged 75 years
dec^d Febuary ye 28th 1695

Here lyes the mortal part of
M R   J O H N   A D A M S
who died Decem^r ye 18 1747
in ye 58 year of his age

> Capt. RICHARD WHELLEN.
> T O M B.

CAPT.   R I C H A R D   W H E L L E N
Died Novr 25th, 1803,
Æ 46.

LT. CALEB CLAPP,
Died at Fort Warren, January, 1815.
Aged 27 years.

NOTE. — The remains of Lt. Caleb Clapp are deposited in the above tomb. He was a lineal descendant of Capt. Roger Clap, whose remains are interred in King's Chapel cemetery, Boston.

Here lyes ye Body of
MR   BENJAMIN   TOMSON
aged 27 years
Dec^d June ye 18th
1 7 3 0

Here lies intered the mortal part of
MRS ABIGAIL JAMES
Consort of Mr Enoch James
who departed this life * * * ye 3^d 1783
Æ 28 years

In Memory of
MR P, R I N C E   C H E W,
who departed this life Octr 21st, 1803,
aged 38 years.

CAPT. JONA. SNELLING'S
T O M B.

JOSHUA SNELLING
son of Capt. Jonathan & Mrs Mary Snelling
died Jan^ry 26 1748
aged 2 years & 2 mo.

Also
S A R A H   S N E L L I N G
died Jan^ry 13th 1749
aged 7 years

Rg 2   Gr 14
J A M E S   P H I L L I P S,
son of Philip and Nancy Taylor,
died May 5, 1818,
aged 6 years.

" Here lies the parent's darling son
Until the bright morning Son arise
To call him up above the skies,
There to enjoy that perfect bliss
In the bright world of happiness."

Here lyes buried the Body of
MR JAMES BOUND
aged 23 years
dec^d Nov ye 6th
1 7 3 8

In Memory of
HENRIETA,
Dau^r of Sarah and Henry Irvalt,
died June 3^d, 1809,
aged 4 years & 4 months.

JEREMIAH MERELLS
aged about 70 years
Dec August ye 25
1 6 7 9

Here lies the Body of
MRS ELIZABETH RUBY
wife to Captⁿ John Ruby
aged 65 years
died Jany 19th 1754

Here lies buried the Body of
MRS ELIZABETH WOTTON
died March 21 1769
* * * d 50 years

JOHN A. GRAHAM,
Child of Ed* Anderson,
died Augst 4, 1818.

Memento Mori
Fugit Hora
Here lyes y^e Body of
JOHN AYRES
aged 62 years & 11 months
who departed this life y^e 12th of August
1 7 1 1

MRS MARY HARVEY
1 7 8 2

Here lyes y^e body of
G R A C E   S T E R L I N G
wife to William Sterling
aged 27 years
Dec^d Feb^{ry} y^e 1st
1 7 2 1 $\frac{}{22}$

In Memory of
MISS ELIZA LONG,
Dau^{tr} of Mr Abraham & Mrs Hannah Long,
who departed this life the
13 of April, 1808,
aged 5 years & 3 months.

Here lies intered y^e body of
C A P T   P E T E R   M O R T I M E R
Brother to Mr James Mortimer
who departed this life Augst 22 1773
aged 59 years
He was born in the city of Waterford in the
Kingdom of Ireland

In Memory of
M R S   M A R Y   H A R V E Y
widow of Capt John Harvey
who died May 2^d 1782
in the 63^d year of her age.

"Mark traveller this humble stone,
Tis death's kind warning to prepare,
Thou too must hasten to the tomb
And mingle with corruption there."

Here lies buried the Body of
CAPT ROGER LUCAS
Born in Oakford
Died March 16th 1772
aged 58 years

Here lies buried the Body of
MRS SARAH LUCAS
wife of Capt Roger Lucas
Died March 26
1 7 6 2
aged 48 years

PETER THOMAS.
TOMB.

Sacred to the Memories of
ANN THOMAS, Obt. Dec. 27, 1796, Æt. 12 days.
ANN R. THOMAS, Obt. May 24, 1804, Æt. 6 years.
SAM^L THOMAS, Obt. Dec. 14, 1805, Æt. 14 months.
Son, still born, Aug. 11, 1806.
ELIZTH K. THOMAS, Obt. May 4, 1821, Æt. 21 years.
MARY THOMAS, Obt. July 7, 1821, Æt. 48 years.

Children and wife of Thomas Kemble Thomas.

In Memory of
MR ALEXANDER LITTLE
who departed this life Sepr ye 25th
1 7 8 5
aged 55 years

S A R A H
Dau[r] to Benjamin & Rebecca Stookas
aged about 11 mo
Dec[d] Aug[t] y[e] 23[d] 1723

J O H N
Son of Mr John and Mrs Dorcas Adams
aged 10 weeks & 6 D[s]
Dec[d] April y[e] 2
1 7 3 7

**S I G O U R N E Y ' S
T O M B.**

Here lyes y[e] Body of
M R   J A M E S   S H I R L E Y
son of Mr John & Mrs Jenet Shirley
who died August y[e] 2[d]
1 7 4 9
in y[e] 31st year of his age

In Memory of
M R   J O H N   J A M E S
who died Dec[r] 22[d]
aged 47 in the year 1803.

```
* * * * * *  worms destroy this body's skin,
* * * * * * *  * *  shall see my Lord —
* * * * * * *  build my body up again
* * * * * * * *  believe his word,
* * * * * *  that lives above the skies —
* * * * * *  safely guard my clay
* * * * * *  shall bid it to arise,
* * * * *  great Judgment day.
```

MARTHA HILLARD
Davghter to Edward & ***** Hillard
aged 2 years & a qvarter
Died Aug^st 21
1 6 8 7

Here lies the Body of
S A R A H   R I T C H E Y
wife of Prince Hall
died Feb the 26th
1 7 6 9
aged 24 years

This stone is sacred to the Memory of

Capt	And of
WILLIAM BURKE	MRS MARY BURKE
who died	wife of
	Capt William Burke
May 24th 1787	who died Jan^ry 15th 1787
Ætat 40	Ætat 38

" They were pleasant in their lives, and in their deaths were
not divided."

Here lyes ye Body of
M R   B E N J A M I N   S N E L L I N G
who died Nov. 6
Anno Dom 1 7 3 9
in y^e 40th year of his age

In Memory of
M R   B E N J^N   D O U B L E D A Y
who departed this life
Sept 2^d 1784
aged 50 years.

Here lyes y^e Body of
MRS ELIZABETH WEBBER
wife to Mr Nathaniel Webber
dec^d March y^e 11th
1 7 3 1 $_{\frac{}{2}}$
in y^e 60 year of her age

In Memory of
MRS SUSANNA HEMMENWAY
wife of Mr Eben^r Hemmenway
& youngest dau^r of Capt Christopher Hoskins
She departed this life
April 17th 1796
in the 34th year of her age

"Here rest the dead, from pain and sorrow free;
She's gone to heaven, O God, to rest with thee;
Her bright example may we make our own,
As far as she in Christ and God was known."

Here lyes buried ye Body of
MR JOSEPH SNELLING
who departed this life
July y^e 1st
1748
aged 53 years 2 months and 10 days

Here lies buried y^e Body of
ANNA SNELLING
Dau^{tr} of Mr Joseph and Mrs Priseila Snelling
who departed this life
Jany the 30th
1766
aged 20 years

THE

ARMS AND TOMB

BELONGING TO THE FAMILY OF

G E E .

In Memory of
E B E N E Z E R W I L D
who departed this life
Decr 4th 1794
in the 37th year of his age
He was a kind husband a tender parent &
sincere Friend

The Family Tomb of
NATHANIEL BARBER Esq.
who lies here deposited,
Died Oct. 14, 1787,
Ætat. 59.

Also,

MRS. ELIZABETH,
wife of Mr. John F. Barber.
Died April 24, 1832,
Æt. 52.

In Memmory of
M R S M A R Y F A R M E R
who died Novr 4th 1798
Ætat 68 years

"Stop here, my friends, and cast an eye;
Remember well that you must die;
Wisely conduct, that so you may
Triumph in Christ at the last day."

In Memory of
MR ABRAHAM HAWARD
who died Nov 11th 1781
aged 22 years

He was a dutiful son, a kind Brother, and
sincere friend

Also
T H O M A S H A W A R D
died Feb 12th 1771
aged 2 years & 5 months

Here lyes intered the Body of
MR WILLIAM PITMAN
aged 45 years
dec^d Decr ye 17th
1 7 3 2.

Here lyes intered the Body of
DEACON JOSIAH LANGDON
who died Novr the 5th
1 7 4 2
in the 55th year of his age

EDW^D LANGDON JUN^R Obt 30th April 1755 Æt 31

NATHANIEL LANGDON Obt 27th Decr 1757 Æt 63

SUSANNA LANGDON Obt 3^d Septr 1760 Æt 65

EPH^M LANGDON A M Obt 21st Novr 1765 Æt 33

DEA^N EDWARD LANGDON Obt 25th May 1766 Æt 69

MARY LANGDON only Child of Edward Langdon Junr
dec^d, Obt 8th Sept 1771 Æt 18

SKILLIN.

Here	Also
Lyes buried y^e	the body of
Body of	MRS JEAN VARNEY
MR JAMES VARNEY	wife of
who died	Mr. James Varney
Jan^{ry} ye 24th	who died April 8th
1752	1752
Aged 74	aged 80

In Memory of
4 Children of Capt John and Mrs Jane Guliker
who are here intered (viz)
JOHN GULIKER Junr who died 23^d Augst 1770
aged 13 days
JOHN GULIKER Junr 7th Augst 1781
aged 14 months
THOMAS GULIKER died 29th June 1783
aged 10 days
MARY GULIKER died 23^d Decr 1784
aged 6 years

| JOHN SMITH'S |
| TOMB. 1812. |

Here	Allso
Lyes the Body of	MRS SUSANNA
MR JOHN HOLLAND	ye wife of Mr John Holland
aged 63 years	aged 60 years
died	died
Sept 9th	July 13th
1 7 3 6	1 7 4 1

Sacred to the Memory of
MRS ELIZABETH KENNEY,
who departed this life Sept 10th,
1 8 0 7 ,
in the 24th year of her age.

" In the cold mansions of the tomb,
How still the solitude ! how deep the gloom !
Here sleeps the dust, unconscious, close confin'd,
But far, far distant dwells the immortal mind."

Here lies buried the Body of
MR ROBERT BALLS
who departed this life Oct 10th
1 7 7 4
in the 75th year of his age

Here lies buried the Body of
MRS MARTHA BALLS
the wife of Mr Robert Balls
who departed this life May 30th
1 7 6 5
aged 82 years

COL. EDWARD PROCTOR.

Here lies buried the Body of
M R   A A R O N   B O A R D M A N
aged 43 years
died Janry ye 9th
1 7 5 4

Sacred to the Memory of
M R   J O H N   G R E E N ,
of this town,
who died May 28th,
1 8 0 6 ,
in the 22d year of his age.

CAPT. JOSEPH INGRAHAM,
died June, 1811.
Æ 48.

Here lies the Body of
MRS PHEBE RICHARDSON
wife of Mr Benjamin Richardson
who departed this life May ye 3^d
1 7 6 8
in the 37th year of her age

Here lyes ye Body of
MRS MARY BASSETT
widow of Mr Francis Bassett
who died Oct^{br} 12th
1 7 4 3
in ye 66th year of her age

ANDREW SIGOURNEY.
TOMB.

Here lyes ye Body of
SAMUEL AVES
Son to Mr Samuel & Mrs Mary Aves
aged 20 years.
dec^d * * *^{r} ye 3^d
1 7 2 7

CAPT. JOHN HARVEY,
died Feby 16th, 1814,
aged 54.

In Memory of
CAPT. NATHANIEL DOAK,
who died Feby 23, 1819,
Æt. 85 years.

> ## SAMUEL HILL
> ## &
> ## EDMUND PARSONS.
> ## TOMB. 1820.
>
> " Lo ! soft remembrance drops the piteous tear,
> " And dearest friendship stands a mourner here."

MRS. ESTHER BADGER, died September 1, 1819,
aged 49 years.

MR. WILLIAM BADGER, died February 2, 1841,
aged 73 years.

MR. EDMUND PARSONS, died September 16, 1837,
aged 49 years.

MR. EDMUND PARSONS, JR., died February 7, 1842,
aged 30 years and 10 months.

JAMES WINCHELL PARSONS, died December 9, 1820,
aged 2 years and 3 months.

MR. NATHANIEL FLETCHER, died * * * *

MRS. FRANCES MARIA BADGER, died Aug., 1844,
aged 35 years.

MR. ALBERT BADGER, died * * * *

MARY B. HARRINGTON, died November 29, 1850,
aged 6 years and 7 months.

CHARLES STEPHEN HILL, aged 2 years.

NATHANIEL H. HILL, aged 1 year.

CHARLES HILL, aged 6 weeks.

MARTHA EMMA BADGER, aged 4 years.

STEPHEN BADGER, aged 1 year.

In Memory of
MISS MARY FITZGEARALD
Daug[r] of Mr Michael & Mrs Honnor Fitzgearald
who died Sept 30th
1 7 8 7
aged 19 years
" Virtue and youth, just in the morning bloom,
With the fair MARY, finds an early tomb."

ICHABOD MACOMBER,
CHARLES HOWARD,
&
EZEKIEL SAWIN'S
Tomb.

MAJOR NATHANIEL HEATH,
died May 5th, 1812,
Ætat. 80.

His wife,
MRS. MARY HEATH,
died Oct. 12th, 1809,
Ætat. 72.

" Grave, the guardian of their dust;
Grave, the treasure of the skies;
Every atom of thy trust
Rests, in hope again to rise.'

Sacred to the Memory of
LT. ROBERT CLARKE,
a native of Boston, N. H.,
who died May 19, A. D. 1813,
Ætat. 34.

Capt. ELIJAH NICKERSON,
&
THOMAS HOPKINS.
1 8 0 4 .

Sacred to the Memory of
CAPT. NATHANIEL GLASIER,
who departed this life
May 27th, in the year of our Lord
1 8 1 2 ,
aged 30 years.
" Long may his grave with rising flowers be drest,
And the green turf lie lightly on his breast."

In Memory of
M R S. S U S A N D U N N ,
wife of Capt. James Dunn,
who died March 1st,
1 8 1 5 ,
Æt. 25.

JOHN COOKSON'S
Tomb.

CAPT. MICHAEL RANDOLS,
died Aug. 11, 1812,
Æt. 45.
" Cease weeping, friends; your flowing tears refrain,—
None can escape from Death's dread, vast domain;
Hush every murmur, check each rising sigh;
Remember all are mortal, born to die."

THOMAS SULLIV**,
JOHN BARBER,
&
JOHN SULLIVAN.

CAPT. THOMAS LAMBERT,
Died May 12th, 1813.
Ætat. 32.

In Memory of
MR. JOSEPH BLAKE,
who died Decr 2, 1805,
Ætat. 26.

Here lies ye Body of
MRS MARCY WILLSON
wife to Mr William Willson
decd Decr ye 15th
1 7 1 9
Ætatis sua 21 years & 7 months

1 7 9 2.
DANIEL INGERSOLL.

Here lies the Body of
MRS ANN THOMAS
wife of Capt William Thomas
who departed this life Novemr 27
1 7 6 7
aged 89 years

HERE LYETH
BURIED Y^E BODY OF
ANN Y^E WIFE OF
JOSEPH. PENWELL AGED
ABOUT 60 YEARS
DECEASED DECEMBER
Y^E 31 1 6 8 8

NATHANIEL BREWER,
ELLIS COOK,
&
GEORGE DARRACOTT'S
TOMB.

**** lyes ye Body **
MR CHRISTOPHER CAPRON
aged 53 years
dec^d Novr ye 14
1 7 2 1

Here lyes ye Body of
MR JOSIAH STONE
aged 62 years & about 5 months
dec^d July 26th
1 7 7 1

In Memory of
MRS. REBECCA CAR,
wife of Mr. John H. Car,
died May 17th, 1805,
Æ 26.

HERE LYETH
BURIED Y^E BODY OF
ANN Y^E WIFE OF
JOSEPH. PENWELL AGED
ABOUT 60 YEARS
DECEASED DECEMBER
Y^E 31 1 6 8 8

NATHANIEL BREWER,
ELLIS COOK,
&
GEORGE DARRACOTT'S
TOMB.

**** lyes ye Body **
MR CHRISTOPHER CAPRON
aged 53 years
dec^d Novr ye 14
1 7 2 1

Here lyes ye Body of
MR JOSIAH STONE
aged 62 years & about 5 months
dec^d July 26th
1 7 7 1

In Memory of
MRS. REBECCA CAR,
wife of Mr. John H. Car,
died May 17th, 1805,
Æ 26.

Here lyeth yᵉ Body of
A B I G A I L   E U E R D E N
yᵉ wife of William Euerden
aged 38 years
decᵈ August 15 1626

NOTE. — The date on this stone, with some others, has been altered. The true date was 1696, as the first settlement of the town was 1630.

> ANN BROWN,
> ELIZABETH HUDSON,
> &
> JOSEPH CALLENDER'S
> TOMB.

Here lyes buried yᵉ Body of
M R S   G R A C E   I R E L A N D
Relict of Capt John Ireland
who died Octᵇʳ 2ᵈ
1 7 3 0
aged 77 years 5 mo & 1 dy

Here lyes yᵉ Body of MR GEORGE WORTHYLAKE who died Novʳ yᵉ 3ᵈ 1718 in yᵉ 45 year of his age	Here lyes yᵉ Body of RUTH Dauʳ of Mr George & Mrs Ann Worthylake who died Novʳ 3ᵈ 1718	Here lyes yᵉ Body of MRS ANN WORTHYLAKE wife of Mr George Worthylake who died Nov 3ᵈ 1718 in yᵉ 40 year her age

NOTE. — Mr. Worthylake, wife, and daughter, were drowned on the Sabbath, in Boston harbor. (*See Appendix.*)

Here lies entombed
the body of
Mrs. Margret Webb,
who died Decr 11th, 1813,
aged 74 years.

<table>
<tr><td>SARAH STONE
Dau^r of Mr William &
Mrs Elizabeth Stone
aged 20 years
Died May 25th
1 7 5 2</td><td>ANNA STONE
Dau^r of Mr William &
Mrs Elizabeth Stone
aged 13 years
Died May 28th
1 7 5 2</td></tr>
</table>

Here lyes y^e Body of
M R T H O M A S H U N T
aged 73 years & 7 months
who dee^d Feb^{ry} y^e 11th
1 7 2 1 $\frac{}{22}$

JABEZ & NATHANIEL
FISHER'S
TOMB.

Sacred to the Memory of
MR. RICHARD ROBERTS,
son to Mr Richard & Mrs Mercy Roberts,
who departed this life
June 16, 1812,
aged 26.

" My glass is run, my life is spent,
My earthly temple was but lent ;
Why should I wish a length of years,
In such a vale of tears ?"

HERE LYES Y͏ᴇ
BOD* OF MRˢ
JUDET COLESWORTHEY
WIFE OF MR GORGE
COLESWORTHEY AGED
TWENTY ONE YEARS
AND THREE MONTHS
AND 25 DAYS OLD
DIED THE 23 DAY
OF APRIL 1729

**MR. THOMAS GOODWILL'S
TOMB.**

Here lies buried
the body of
Mʀ Tʜᴏᴍᴀs Gᴏᴏᴅᴡɪʟʟ
aged 62 years
who died Decʳ 21ˢᵗ 1749

Here lyes buried the Body of
MRS MERCY STODDARD
wife to Mr Anther Stoddard
aged 26 years
Decᵈ Febʳʸ yᵉ 14ᵗʰ
1 7 3 8

Erected in Memory of
MR THOMAS WEBB
Son of Mr Nehemiah & Mrs Sarah Webb
* * * * *

HERE LIES BURIED THE BODY OF

MAJOR JOHN RUDDOCK, ESQ.,

Deceased September 2^d, 1772, aged 59 years and 2 ^{mo}.

He was in commission of the Peace
and Justice of the Court and County of Suffolk 13 yrs ;
He commanded his Majesty's North Battery in Boston
13 yrs ;
And was selectman for the same town 9 yrs.
Could a heart that felt, and a hand that relieved, the
miseries attendant upon humanity —
Could the truest patriotism,
equally superior
to the frowns of power and the rage of party,
which with invincible constancy
asserted and defended universally
(for he was a citizen of the world)
the rights of mankind —
Could undeviating integrity
in every office
which he dignified by holding,
joined to the most impartial
dispensation of justice —
In fine,
Could extensive virtue or distinguished worth

rescue from the tomb,

Reader,

thou hadst not been told

Here lies Ruddock.

Depart!

Imitate his virtues,

and with him

merit the eulogium of thy country.

Time may efface this monumental stone,
But time nor malice can his worth dethrone
For villains living oft may buy a name,
But virtue only swells posthumous fame.

In Memory of
C A P T   C A L E B   H A Y D E N
died on the 2ᵈ day of July
Anno Domini 1795
in the 57ᵗʰ year of his age

" The monumental stone, by many read,
In pensive numbers, praise the silent dead ;
But learn that virtue softens every pain ;
To live in glory, IMITATE the MAN
Who died to save, and dying, can restore
Your rescued souls to praise HIM evermore."

Here lies buried the Body of
C A P T   R I C H A R D   W A T T S
aged 30 years.
Died March yᵉ 8ᵗʰ
1 7 4 9 $\frac{50}{}$

> **JAMES BARTLETT,**
> **JOHN THAYER,**
> **JOSEPH URANN'S**
> **TOMB. 1811.**

In Memory of
MR. JOHN NELSON,
who departed this life May 5th,
1 8 0 6,
aged 46 years.

Here lyes y^e Body of
M R S J O A N N A H U N T
wife to Mr Ephraim Hunt
aged about 52 years
dec^d August 20th
1 7 3 1.

> **EDWARD BELL'S**
> **TOMB.**

In Memory of
J A M E S B. S M I T H,
died June 17th, 1805,
Æ. 48.

Also, his wife,
S U S A N N A H S M I T H,
died March 25th, 1809,
Æ. 57.

```
┌─────────────────────────────┐
│  JOSHUA    │   JOHN F.      │
│  LORING.   │   NEWTON.      │
│         18 │ 19.            │
└─────────────────────────────┘
```

Here lies buried the Body of
M R S   S A R A H   B U T L E R
wife to Mr Joseph Butler
died Octr 25th
1 7 5 4
aged 38 years & 7 months

In Memory of
J O H N   C A P E N
the son of Mr Hopestill & Mrs Patience Capen
who died Feb 19th
1 7 7 0
aged 7 years.

```
┌─────────────────────────────┐
│   ASAHEL  STOCKWELL         │
│            &                │
│   D A N I E L  W I S E .    │
└─────────────────────────────┘
```

In Memory of
I S A A C   H O W A R D   D A V I S ,
only child of John & Elizth Davis,
died May 8th,
1 8 0 7 ,
Æ. 20 Mo^s & 8 days.

"Sleep, sleep, sweet babe, death's done no harm,
Christ Jesus calls thee to his arms."

| MICHAEL DALTON |
| AND |
| WILLIAM F. CLARK. |
| TOMB. |

Here lies buried the Body of
M R S A N N C O P I N G
aged 62 years.
Dec^d Augt ye 26
1 7 3 1

CHARLES GYLES
son to Mr Edward & Mrs Elizabeth Gyles
died May 16th 1754
aged 5 years

Here lyes intered the Body of
MR JOHN PULLEN
Dec^d Jany y^e 9th
1 7 1 7
in y^e 61st year of his age

| SIMEON BOYDEN'S |
| TOMB. 1825. |

Here lyes the Body of
M R S M A R Y P U L L E N
wife to Capt John Pullen
aged 56 years
died March y^e 4th
1 7 1 2 $_{\frac{12}{13}}$

> NATHANIEL NOTTAGE
> &
> JONATHAN LORING, JR.
> TOMB. 1828.

Here lyes y^e Body of
S A M U E L   B A D C O C K
died Octr y^e 24th
1 7 2 1
in y^e 31st year of his age

Sacred to the Memory of
M R S. L U C Y P A R R Y,
wife of Mr Richard Parry,
who departed this life Sep^t 23^d,
A. D. 1800,
in the **th year of her age.
Also
her son
C O R N E L I U S C O O K
died Nov 2^d
1 7 9 1

> DAVID MARDEN'S
> TOMB. 1828.

JOHN PRICHARD
son to Mr William & Mrs Atterlanter Prichard
died March 17th
1 7 5 7
aged 14 years 3 months & 13 days

```
THOMAS  GREEN
&
JOHN  LEWIS'S
TOMB.  1819.
```

In Memory of
ABIGAIL ALLCOCK
dau^r of Mr Robert & Mrs Abigail Allcock
died Octr 26th
1 7 8 4
aged 19 months

Here lyes ye Body of
M R J O S E P H P R A T T
deceased August ye 27th
1 7 1 9
& buried Sep^{tr} ye 11th
in ye 30th year of his age

```
TURELL  TUTTLE'S
TOMB.  1801.
```

Here lyes buried the Body of
MARY BOUTCHER
dau^r to Deacon Thomas & Mrs Ann Boutcher
died Sept 2^d
1 7 6 7
" Some hearty friend may drop a tear
On these dry bones, and say,
These limbs were active once like thine,
But thine must be as they."

WILLIAM McCLENNEN
&
JOSEPH JONES.

TOMB. 1812.

Sacred to the Memory of
CAPT. JAMES SMITH,
who departed this life
July 1st,
1 8 0 3 ,
aged 43 years.

Here lyes ye body of
MRS ELIZABETH SMITH
widow to Mr Thomas Smith
who died Janry 23d
1 7 5 3
aged 75 years.

JOSIAH MARSHALL'S

TOMB. 1812.

In Memory of
GEORGE WARDELL,
youngest son of Capt. John Wardell,
who died Decr 5th,
1 8 0 2 ,
aged 2 years and 7 months.

" Here rest sweet innocence and love,
His soul is fled to joys above."

FAC ET SPERA.

"FEBRUARY 170⁰⁄₁

BE IT REMEMBERED THAT ON THE 14ᵀᴴ OF THE MONTH

DIED IN BOSTON

THE AGED AND REVᴰ.

MR. THOMAS THORNTON,

FORMERLY MINISTER OF YARMOUTH,

BUT BY REASON OF AGE

INCAPABLE OF THAT SERVICE."

Pemberton's MS. Journal.

ROBERT KING,
son of Mr Henry & Mrs Sarah King
aged 13 months & 9 days,
dec^d Sept 19th
1 7 4 *

---

*RASMUS
son to Erasmus & Persis Stevens
aged 2 years
deceased Novr ye 1st
1 7 2 1

This stone perpetuates the memory of
MRS ELIZABETH HERMAN
wife of Mr Leopold F Herman
who departed this life
June 5th
1 7 9 7
aged 20

" An angel's arm can't snatch her from the grave; legions of
angels can't confine her there."

Also
their daughter
E L I Z A
aged 5 mo & 13 days
died July 24th
1 7 9 6

" Sleep, sweet babe, and take thy rest,
God called thee home ; He thought it best."

Here lies ye Body of
G E O R G E H I L L E R
aged about 32 years
died August ye 22^d
1 7 2 1

BENJ., AMOS, JOSHUA,
&
JOHN BINNEY'S
TOMB.

Here lies intered the mortal part of
MR EDWARD PAGE
who departed this life
November the 10th
1 7 8 4
aged 68 years

Here lyes ye Body of
M R S R A C H E L Y O U N G
wife to Mr An**ony Young
who died Nov^{br} 1st
1 7 3 2
in ye 49th year of her age

ABRAHAM MILLET.
TOMB. 1821.

In Memory of
CHARLOTTE GOULD,
daughter of James & Sally Gould,
who died Aug. 26th,
1 8 0 5 ,
aged 19 months & 10 days.
"Sleep, sleep, sweet babe, and take thy rest,
God called thee home, he thought it best."

> ADAMS BAILEY,
> SAMUEL NOYSE,
> MARCY BLANCHARD.
> TOMB. 1821.

In Memory of
MRS ELIZABETH HAYDEN
consort of Capt Caleb Hayden
who departed this life
September 23ᵈ
1 7 9 0
aged 55 years
"Here rest the dead, from pain and sorrow free;
Her soul in heaven, to live, O God, with thee;
Her bright example may we make our own,
As far as she in Christ and God was known."

SARAH
Daughter of John & Jane Snelling
aged 12 years 10 mo & 17 Ds
died december yᵉ 17
1 7 0 2

> DAVIS WHITMAN.
> 1804.

*n Memory of
WILLIAM
son of Mr William Mills & Mrs Betsey his wife
he was drowned August the 25ᵗʰ
1 7 9 *
in the 6ᵗʰ year of his age

NOAH LINCOLN
&
JONATHAN THAXTER'S
TOMB. 1812.

This stone is erected in Memory of
MISS POLLY TIDMARSH BARKER
who died Sept 24th,
1 7 9 8
aged 17 years
" Sleep on, dear youth, God saw it best,
To waft you to eternal rest."

In Memory of
MISS ELIZA,
eldest daughter of Mr. William Mills & Mrs. Betsey,
his wife,
died August 20th, 1809,
Æ. 17 years & 6 mos.

RUFUS BAXTER,
ELIZA STEPHENS.
1 8 2 1 .

In Memory of
CAPT. JOHN CROZER,
who died April 27th,
1 8 0 1 ,
aged 42 years.
" Oft as thy friends shall tarry here,
To drop upon thy grave a tear,
While sweet remembrance swells her breast,
She'll bid thy gentle spirit rest."

SAMUEL HICHBORN, JR.,
&
GEDNEY KING'S
TOMB. 1812.

Here lies intered the Body of
ELIZABETH LANE
consort to Capt Ebenezer Lane
who departed this life 12th Nov^r
1 7 8 1
in the 33^d year of his age.

Here lies buried the Body of
MRS SUSANNAH TOMSON
the wife of Capt Thomas Thomson
who departed this life
October ye 10th
1 7 4 7
in the 27th year of his age

THOMAS CAPEN.
TOMB. 1811.

In Memory of
MISS NANCY GREEN,
youngest daughter of Mr. Thomas and Mrs. Mary
Green,
who died Dec. 18, 1800.
aged 11 years.
" Retire, my friends, dry up your tears,
I must lie here till Christ appears."

HENRY CLAP

&

JONATHAN FORBS.

TOMB. 1819.

Sacred to the Memory of
MRS. ELIZABETH FERNALD,
amiable wife of Capt. Abraham Fernald,
(also in memory of her husband and children,)
who died Feby. 27th,
1804,
in the 34th year of her age.

O, my friends, remember that the Lord giveth, and the Lord taketh away, and blessed be the name of the Lord. O, my husband and children, dry up your tears, and remember that you must all follow me sooner or later, where we must all lie till Christ our Saviour bids us arise ; for thy will must be done. Amen.

ELIJA L. GREEN.

Here lies the Body of
MR PETER HAVVATT
aged 42 years
Dec^d Feby 20th
1739 $\frac{40}{40}$

Here lies buried the infant son
of Mr Eben & Mrs Phebe Lane
born and died Decr 8th
1780

EZRA HAWKES
&
THOMAS GOULD.
TOMB. 1812.

He** **** Bur*** the body of
MR JONATHAN BROWN
who died June y^e 14th
1 7 4 6
in y^e 63^d year of his age

Here lies buried the Body of
POLLY ROBINS
Dau^tr of Mr James & Mrs Susanna Robins
died March 28
1 7 7 8
aged 6 years

T. OLIVER.

Sacred to the Memory of
CAPTAIN JONATHAN CARY,
who departed this life Decr. 29th,
Anno Domini 1801,
aged 85 years.

A full believer in the universal religion.

" Why do we mourn departed friends,
Or shrink at death's alarms ?
'Tis but the voice that Jesus sends,
To call us to his arms."

GEORGE LOW
&
ABIAH P. LOW.
TOMB. 1836.

ABIAH P. LOW,
died May 28th, 1846,
aged 51 years, 7 months.

This Stone is erected in Memory of
CAPT CALEB HOPKINS JUNR
who died Octbr 19th
1 7 9 1
in the 39th year of his age

Here lies buried the Body of
MRS SUSANNAH SOMES
the wife of Capt Nehemiah Somes
died Sept 3d 1770
aged 23 years

CLARK.

Here lies buried the Body of
MRS SUSANNA WHITE
wife of Mr John White
died June 4th
1 7 6 9
aged 48 years

ROSS,
FAMILY TOMB.

And^w Ross, died Novr 1st, 1814, Æ. 37.
Wm Ross, died April 1st, 1816, Æ. 42.
John Ross, died April 5th, 1841, Æ. 64.
Marg^t Ross, died Jan. 20, 1846, Æ. 72.

Here lies the Body of
BETSEY HOPKINS
Dau^{tr} of Michael & Joanna Hopkins
died Augst 29th
1 7 8 3
aged 15 months & 17 days

SARAH DODGE
Dau^r to Mr James & Mrs Mary Dodge
aged 13 months
died May 4th
1 7 4 8

W. SHERBURNE.

Here lies the Body of
ELIZABETH BALLARD
the wife of Mr Samuel Ballard
who departed this life March the 16th
1 7 7 6
aged 45 years

```
ISAAC S. TOMPKINS
AND
JOSIAH BROWN.
1845.
```

In Memory of
MRS NABBY DODGE
wife of Capt James Dodge
who departed this life March 28th 1796
aged 25 years

Here was buried
MRS FANNY DISSMORE
wife of Capt Thomas Dissmore
who lived 35 years & died the 29th of December
1 7 8 8
it being the anniversary of her Bi***
"The living when the ****** ***** ***."

```
B. HENDERSON.
```

Here lies buried the Body of
CAPT THOMAS EELES
aged 55 years
died Novr ye 16th 1748

Here lies ye Body of
MRS ELIZABETH HUBBARD
who died Feby ye 5th 1758 *** ***

MR. JOHN FENNO
&
CAPT. JOHN HOWE'S
TOMB. 1819.

Here lies buried the Body of
CAP^T WILLIAM TREFRY
aged 56 years
died May ye 6th
1 7 6 1

" Stop, O youth, and kindly drop a tear,
A youth once gay like you, lies buried here.

Here lies buried the remains of
JOHN SCHOLLAY
son of James Schollay & Susanna his wife
who died Nov ye 17th
1 7 6 3
aged 10 years
" His body's here, his soul to heaven is gone,
Then to receive from God its righteous doom."

S. PRENTISS.

Sacred to the memory of
MRS MARCY HAMMATT
wife of Capt Benjamin Hammatt
who died Jany 6th
1 7 9 6
aged 69 years

A   D   1 8 1 1.

J. PIERCIVAL.   N. PARKER.

" All are but part of one stupendous whole,
Whose body nature is, and God the soul."

JOSEPH YOUNG
son of William Young
died Octr 3^d 1731
aged 1 month & 9 days

MRS. ELIZABETH HAMMOND,
died April 15,
1 8 1 0 ,
aged 45 years.

" To heavenly realms of endless peace,
Angels her patient soul have borne,
To taste pure joys that never cease,
With Father, Holy Ghost, and Son."

WARD JACKSON
&
HEMAN LINCOLN'S
TOMB. 1819.

In Memory of
MRS SUSANNAH FOSTER
wife of Mr Jonathan Foster
died Octr 15
1 7 9 4
** years

J. & M. HALL.

Sacred to the Memory of
JOSEPH HOWARD, ESQ.,
who died July 20, 1808,
Æ 54.

" If love of him you wish to show,
 Like him aspire to be ;
So in some happier land at last,
 Your friend you yet may see,
When the great Shepherd sounds his call,
 And all the dead arise."

T. & J. LEWIS.

**** *ies the body of
*ILLIAM MELLENS
parted this life * ye 10th
1 7 5 5
** **e 48th year ** his age

Here lies the Body of
MRS KATHERIN HOSKINS
wife of Capt Christopher Hoskins
died Janry 5th 1769
aged 34 years

BASSETT.

W I L L I A M
&
J O H N H O W E ' S
T O M B. 1 8 2 0.

Here lies the Body of
MRS MARY POOLE
aged 50 years
Dec^d July 28th
1 7 3 7

Here lies buried the Body of
LYDIA PARSONS
widow of the late Revd Jonathan Parsons
of Newbury Port
departed this life April 17th
1 7 7 8
aged 47 years

F R A N C I S M A S S E,
L E O N A R D S P A U L D I N G,
J O H N G A L E ' S
T O M B.

In Memory of
MRS HANNAH YOUNG
widow of Mr William Young
died Oct 13th
1 7 9 0
aged 87 years

ALEXR. VANNEVAR
&
JACOB BARSTOW'S
TOMB. 1819.

Here lies the Body of
M R J A M E S D O D G E
who died Novr ye 24th
1 7 5 9
aged 46 years

JOHN WYERS.
TOMB. 1820.

Here lies buried the Body of
M R S A M U E L S P R I N G
died April 6th
1 7 5 2
in the 22^d year of his age

Here lies buried ye Body of
MR RICHARD BRADBURN
Son of Mr Joseph Bradburn of London
who departed this life
Jan^{ry} 2^d 1739
in ye 21st year of his age

EDMUND WINCHESTER.
TOMB. 1819.

In Memory of
J O H N   M I L K,
who died July 11th, 1808,
aged 43 years.
He was valued in life, and died lamented.

Also
J A M E S
died July 16th 1792
Æ 14 ds
E L E A N O R
died Nov 7th 1794
Æ 14 mº & 17 ds
S U S A N N A H
died Augt 4th 1802
Æ 7 years.
Children of Mr John & Mrs Eleanor Milk

JAMES SHERMAN'S
Family Tomb.

In Memory of
M A R Y   A N N,
only daugh of Mr William & Mrs Mary Ann Homer,
died April 1, 1816,
Æt. 4 years & 4 months.
" Cropt as a bud from yonder tree,
She's gone to rest, from trouble free."

Here lyes ye Body of
A N N A   B U R R I L L
died Oct 7th 1773
aged 10 months

Here lies yᵉ body of
MARY BURRILL
Daughᵗ of Samuel Burrill & Mary his wife
died April 5ᵗʰ 1777
aged 9 years & 6 months

Here lyes yᵉ Body of
SARAH NORTON
wife to David Norton
aged 49 years
decᵈ October 30ᵗʰ, 1721

Here lyes the body of
MRS JANE BURRIL
wife to Mr Joseph Burril
who died Janʸ 20ᵗʰ
1 7 4 0 ,
aged 46 years.

JOSIAH SNELLING'S
TOMB.

Her* **** *****d th* **** of
MR JOHN LANGDON
aged 82 years
decᵈ Decʳ yᵉ 6ᵗʰ 1732

Here lies intered the Body of
MRS JOANNA FEVERYEAR
wife to Mr Grafton Feveryear
aged 33 years
decᵈ April yᵉ 10ᵗʰ
1 7 7 2

DANIEL
&
SAMUEL ADAMS.
TOMB. 1813.

MRS. SUSAN,
wife of Samuel Adams,
died Jany 25th, 1813,
aged 27.

Here lyes ye Body of
MR JOSEPH CROWLLEY
who died March 6th
Anno Dom 1738 9
aged 69 years

In Memory of
MRS REBECCA YOUNG,
who died March 29,
1 8 0 8,
aged 79 years.

CAPT. WILLIAM WARD'S
TOMB.

Here lyes ye Body of
MRS MARGARET FLETCHER
wife of Mr William Fletcher
aged 55 years
died Feb^{ry} ye 9th
1 7 4 7 8

```
ROBERT BARBER'S
TOMB. 1811.
```

***UEL HEATH
aged 7 years and 3 mo
died May 23^d 1752

D E B O R A H   H E A T H
Æ 12 years
died Jan^{ry} 7th 1753 —
The children of Mr Saml & Mrs Elizth Heath

```
JOSEPH
AUSTIN.
TOMB.
```

Here lies the Body of
M R   J O H N   W H I T E
aged 63 years
died Dec y^e 1st 1746

Also
the body of

MRS KATHERINE WHITE
wife to Mr John White
aged 60 years
Died Feb^{ry} y^e 3^d
1 7 4 6 $_7$

```
JACOB RHOADES
TOMB.
```

```
┌──────────────────────────────────┐
│  WILLIAM  HALL                   │
│         &                        │
│  CORNELIUS B. SIMMONS.           │
│     TOMB.  1819.                 │
└──────────────────────────────────┘
```

Here lies buried yᵉ Body of
MR ALEXANDER SCAMMELL
who departed this life
December 27ᵗʰ
1 7 6 6
in the 64 year of his age

Here lies the body of
MRS MARY SCAMMELL
wife of Mr Alexander Scammell
who died August the 15ᵗʰ
1 7 6 0
aged 57 years

```
┌──────────────────────────────────┐
│  WILLIAM  BADGER                 │
│         &                        │
│  THOMAS  RICHARDSON'S            │
│     TOMB.  1842.                 │
└──────────────────────────────────┘
```

Here lies buried the Body of
MR NATHANIEL BROWN
son of Mr Nathaniel & Mrs Mary Brown
died Decʳ 8ᵗʰ
1 7 5 9
in the 23ᵈ year of his age

FRANCIS HOLMES
&
BENJ. CUSHING'S
TOMB. 1819.

Here lies buried the Body of
MRS MARY BROWN
widow of Mr Nathaniel Brown
died March 5th 1780

Here lies buri** the body of
MRS ANN BROWN
widow of Mr William Brown
died Sept 1st 1751
aged 74

UTLEY, HEATH,
RAYNER, REED,
AND BAKER'S
TOMB. 1842.

Here lies buried the Body of
MR WILLIAM BROWN
died June the 4th
1 7 4 5
in the 74th year of his age

JOSEPH WHEELEN.
TOMB. 1820.

> **E B E N   G A Y**
> **&**
> **E L I   V E A Z I E ' S**
> **T O M B. 1 8 1 9.**

Here lies buried the Body of
M R S   A N N   B R O W N
wife to Willm Brown
aged about 57 years
dec^d March ye 31st 1731

Here lies ye Body of
J O H N   B R O W N
son of William and Anne Brown
aged 21 years & 3 m°
dec^d Octo^br 14
I 7 2 1

> **BRADLE CUMINGS**
> **&**
> **SIMON W. ROBINSONS**
> **T O M B.**

Here lyes ye Body of
MARY MOORE
daugh^tr of Capt Richard & Mrs Mary Moore
of Oxford
who dec^d May y^e 27th
1 7 3 0
aged 19 years

> NATHANIEL PARKER'S
> T O M B . 1828.

Here lies yᵉ Body of
C A P T J A M E S D E N N E N
aged 40 years 4 months & 3 days
died August 11ᵗʰ
1 7 5 7

Here lyes yᵉ body of
MR JOHN CADWELL
aged 66 years
Decᵈ Janʸ yᵉ 2ᵈ
$1732\frac{}{3}$

> THOMAS FROTHINGHAM
> AND OTHERS.
> T O M B . 1819.

D O R Y T H Y
G R E E N O V G H
A G E D 4 Y E A R S
& 8 M O N T H S
D Y E D Y ᴱ 2 0
O C T O B E R
1 6 6 7

> JAMES DAVIS.
> TOMB. 1821.

16 *

NO. 2.

EBENEZER SHUTE
AND
JONATHAN TURNER'S
FAMILY TOMB. 1806.

Deposited here : —

EBEN'R. SHUTE, born in Malden, Jan. 5, 1775 ; died in Boston, May 23, 1850.

SUSANNAH SHUTE, (his wife,) born in Hingham, Nov. 22, 1773 ; died in Boston, Feb. 1, 1847.

And their children and grand-children : —

CALEB B. SHUTE, born July 7, 1806 ; died April 4, 1840.

JOSEPH B. SHUTE, born April 28, 1808 ; died June 15, 1840.

SUSAN G. STETSON, (wife of Joshua Stetson,) born June 9, 1815 ; died August 9, 1844.

FRANCES, (child of Eben'r. Shute, Jr.,) born Jan. 17, 1832 ; died Oct. 7, 1836.

FRANCES, (child of Eben'r. Shute, Jr.,) born May 27, 1838 ; died August 31, 1838.

SUSAN, (child of Caleb B. Shute,) born April 5, 1836 ; died August 26, 1839.

SARAH STETSON, (child of James M. Shute,) born May 14, 1844 ; died the same day.

SUSAN STETSON, (child of James M. Shute,) born Oct. 5, 1845 ; died May 8, 1846.

MRS. RACHEL YOUNG.

N I C H O L A S
V P S H A L L   A G E D
A B O V T   7 0   Y E A R S
D Y E D   Y^E * * * *   O F
A V G U S T   1 6 7 7

ROBERT RIPLEY'S
TOMB. 1824.

J O S E P H
C O C K E
A G E D   4 6   Y E A R S
D E C^D J A N U A R Y
Y^E 1 5   1 6 7 $\frac{8}{9}$

GEORGE VANNEVAR.
TOMB. 1845.

SAMUEL RHODES
son to William Rhodes and Mary his wife
who died Octr 9th
1 7 5 9
aged 12 years & 4 months

> ELIZA WAKEFIELD
> &
> HENRY GOODRICH'S
> TOMB. 1811.

Here lies buried yᵉ Body of
MR ROBERT DUNCAN
Merchᵗ
who departed this life
January yᵉ 24ᵗʰ
1 7 5 2
in the 50 year of his age

> J. GREENOGH.

Here lies buried the Body of
MRS ISABELLA DUNCAN
wife to Mr Robert Duncan
who departed this life
Febʸ 2ᵈ
1 7 4 9 $\frac{}{50}$
in yᵉ 38ᵗʰ year of her age

> CAPT. SAMUEL NICHELS
> &
> MR. JESSE KINGSBURY'S
> TOMB. 1825.

> ROBERT THOMPSON
> &
> JOHN WADE.
> 1811.

Here lyes y^e Body **
MRS PATIENCE STARLING
wife to Mr William Starling Junr
who died June 2^d 1760
aged 40 years

Also
JOHN STARLING
their son
died Sept 1st 1760
aged 14 years

> NATH'L., JOHN,
> &
> CHARLES WELLS.
> TOMB. 1811.

Here lyes buried the Body of
MRS BRIGET LAD
departed this life Novr ye 2^d
1 7 4 3
in the 79 year of her age

> AMASA WINCHESTER'S
> TOMB. 1815.

EDWARD & JOHN
SARGENT,
&
ANN BURCHISTED'S
TOMB. 1820.

Here lies ye Body of
MRS HANNAH PIERCE
wife of Mr Samuel Pierce
who departed this life May 7th
1 7 8 4
aged 46 years

Here lyes ye Body of
MRS MARY PIERCE
wife of Mr Jonathan Pierce of Charlestown
aged 81 years
Died Decr ye 18th
1 7 4 4

ELLIOT, KIMBLE,
&
PRATT'S
TOMB. 1819.

Here lies ye Body of
GRACE PALMER
wife to Mr George Palmer
who departed this life June ye 5th
1 7 5 0
aged 45 years

ISAAC JENKINS,

LUTHER FELTON,

EARL GODDARD,

&

SOLON JENKINS.

TOMB. 1821.

In Memory of
JOSEPH HAMMATT
obt Feb^ry 19th 1798
Æ 48

In Memory of
MR JOHN POLLEY
son of Mr Simeon and Mrs Mary Polley
who died Octr 3^d
1 7 8 7
in the 23^d year of his age
" May guardian cherubs watch their sacred trust,
Till recent life reanimate his dust."

WILLIAM HARTT'S
TOMB.

In Memory of
MRS. SARAH CHAMPNEY,
wife of Capt. Caleb Champney,
died Octr 13th,
1 8 0 0.
" The joys of faith triumphant rise,
And wing the soul above the skies."

```
┌─────────────────────────────┐
│                             │
│   ANDREW  J.  ALLEN         │
│          AND                │
│   THOMAS MICKELL'S          │
│        TOMB.                │
│                             │
└─────────────────────────────┘
```

In Memory of
MRS. MARTHA CABOT,
who departed this life on Saturday, March 11th,
1 8 0 9 ,
aged 60 years.

" So unafflicted, so composed a mind,
So firm, yet soft, so young, yet so refined,
Wasting disease and pain severely tried —
The saint sustained it, but the woman died."

Also
In Memory of
MR. GEORGE CABOT,
who departed this life on Sunday, Feby 5th,
1 8 0 4 ,
aged 20 years,

After a long and distressing sickness, which he bore
with meekness and resignation, in hope of
a glorious immortality.

```
┌─────────────────────────────┐
│   SAMUEL  WINSLOW'S          │
│      TOMB.  1826.           │
└─────────────────────────────┘
```

In Memory of
DEA^N SAMUEL HOLLAND
who died August 17th 1798
Æ 98

NATHANIEL HAMMOND
&
O. & S. DAVIS.
TOMB. 1819.

In Memory of
MR WILLIAM POLLEY
son of Mr Simeon & Mrs Mary Polley
Died Decr 20th
1782
in the 24th year of his age

BARKER EMERSON, JUN.,
&
WARNER CLAFLIN'S
TOMB. 1815.

In Memory of
MRS ANN BEERS
widow of Mr William Beers
who departed this life Decr 18th
1784
aged 79 years

S. YENDAELL'S
TOMB. 1816.
AND
THOMAS HUDSON'S.

```
PETER  BRIGHAM'S
AND
ANDREW  HARRINGTON'S
TOMB.  1814.
```

Sacred to the Memory of
CALEB DINSDAL CHAMPNEY,
Obt. Oct. 4th, 1802,
Æ. 26.

"To part with worth invaluable ; to feel regret mantled in
sympathy ; to lose the richest treasure Heaven bestows ;
to realize the agonizing pang of separation ; still to
bear misfortune's cruel lash, is the lot of man :
but resignation tempers every scene, and
points our warmest, fondest hopes to
heaven."

```
NATH'L. FAXON'S
TOMB.  1814.
```

SAMUEL WHITEHEAD
son of Samuel & Mary Whitehead
aged 1 year 6 months and 22 days
Dec^{d} August 26th
1 7 1 9

```
CAPT.  SAMUEL  EAMES
AND
GEORGE  REDDING'S
TOMB.  1811.
```

BENJAMIN SWEETSER
&
ENOCH H. SNELLING.
TOMB.

Here lyes ye Body of
MRS MARY HUGHES
dau^r of Mr Richard & Mrs Sarah Hughes
who died March ye 7th
1 7 6 5
aged 46 years
" Time, what an empty vapor 'tis ! and days, how swift they fly !
Our life is ever on the wing, and death is ever nigh ;
The moment when our life begins, we all begin to die."

EBEN FROTHINGHAM'S
TOMB. 1814.

Here lies y^e Body of
SARAH BENNIT
wife to Samuel Bennit
aged 75 years
dec^d January y^e 18
1 6 8 $\frac{2}{3}$

JOHN H. PRAY
&
J. G. L. LIBBY'S
TOMB. 1832.

RANSFORD
&
FARRINGTON'S
TOMB. 1814.

CAPT. JOHN SUTER
&
FRANCIS WALKER'S
TOMB. 1811.

In ****** **
MR. JO*****
who depar*** **** ****
April 27th, 18**.

Also
MISS NANCY ******
who departed **** ****
August 10th, 1800,
aged **.

" Mouldering to dust here lies ***
Of two happy spirits gone to joy **
Where peace sits smiling on th**
And brightens every feature by**."

FAMILY TOMB OF
DANIEL DICKENSON,
who died June 23,
1 8 4 5 ,
Æt. 72 years.

HIRAM SMITH,
FAMILY TOMB.

Sacred to the Memory

OF

WILLIAM SULLIVAN SMITH,

OBT. FEB. 2, 1816, AGED 17 DAYS.

HIRAM SMITH,

OBT. AUG. 28, 1817, AGED 6 MONTHS.

HIRAM SHURTLEFF SMITH,

OBT. APRIL 29, 1818, AGED 11 HOURS.

JULIA ANN SMITH,

OBT. JUNE, 4, 1821, AGED 8 WEEKS.

BENJAMIN SHURTLEFF SMITH,

OBT. MAY 4, 1824, AGED 5 MONTHS, 14 DAYS.

BENJAMIN SHURTLEFF SMITH,

OBT. AUG. 22, 1834, AGED 12 MONTHS.

" Ere sin could blight, or sorrow fade,
Death came with friendly care,
The opening buds to heaven conveyed,
And bade them blossom there."

𝕮𝖍𝖗𝖎𝖘𝖙'𝖘 𝕮𝖍𝖚𝖗𝖈𝖍.

CAPT. THOMAS POTTS'
TOMB.

Here lyes entomb^d the body of the
REV TIMOTHY CUTLER D D
First minister of this church

deceased Augst 17 1765

aged 81 years

Also

the body of

MRS ELISATH CUTLER

widow of the above

died Septr ye 12th 1771

aged 81 years

Also

the body of

* * * *   * * * *

SHUBAEL BELL & ROBERT FENNLLY.
1808.

HEIRS OF THE REV. DR. WALTER,

deceased, viz. :

L Y N D E   W A L T E R ,

W I L L I A M   W A L T E R ,

N A T H ᴸ   S M I T H ,

J O H N   O D I N .

1 8 0 8 .

MRS. MARY OTHEMAN,

died 12th April, 1802, Æ. 45.

A. OTHEMAN, JUNᴿ.,

her son, died 18th Feby 1805, Æ. 21.

MRS. HANNAH OTHEMAN,

died 4th Janʳy, ****, Æ. 31.

EDWARD MᶜREDDING,

died 10th June, 1808, Æ. 10 months.

GODFREY M. IBONE,

died April 30th 1815, aged 39.

ANTHONY OTHEMAN,

died Feby 9, 1835, aged 85 years.

HENRY OTHEMAN,

died May 25, 1838, aged 47 years.

BELONGING TO

MR. THOS. CARNES & MR. JOSEPH WHEELWRIGHT.

Here lies the bodies of

MR SAMUEL WEEKS

died August 11th 1740

aged 49

MADAM ELIZATH WHEELWRIGHT

consort to the Hon John Wheelwright Esq

died Feb^{ry} 23^d 1748

Æ 45

Mr Weeks designed this tomb for his friends.

Appendix.

Capt. Thomas Lake. (p. 2.)

ACCORDING to Betham's Baronetage, Captain Lake was of the ninth generation in descent from John Lake, of Normanton, in Yorkshire, Esquire, who was of the fifth generation from Sir William Caley, of Owby, Knight, only son of Hugh de Caley, of Owby, County of Norfolk, (who died in 1286,) by his wife, Agnes, daughter and heiress of Hamo de Hamsted.

Captain Lake was son of Richard Lake, of Irby, in Lincolnshire, and brother of Sir Edward Lake, LL. D., Baronet, Advocate General of the Kingdom of Ireland, Chancellor of the Diocese of Lincoln, &c., who died July 18, 1674, aged seventy-seven, and lies buried in the Cathedral of Lincoln, leaving his title and estate to his nephew, Thomas, son of Capt. Lake. John, a brother of Sir Edward and Capt. Thomas, was living in Boston in 1676. Capt. Lake's wife, who survived him, was Mary, daughter of Hon. Stephen Goodyear,

Deputy Governor of New Haven Colony, who died in London, 1658. He came to New England, a man of fortune, and was extensively engaged in commercial pursuits. He was associated with some of the earliest English proprietors of lands in New Hampshire and Maine. While attending to the affairs of the "Kennebec purchase," in 1676, he was slain by the Indians. His sons were educated in England. Thomas, born in Boston, Feb. 9, 1656, an Utter Barrister of the Honorable Society of the Middle Temple, London, died 22d May, 1711, aged 55, and lies buried in the Middle Temple, London.

Capt. Lake's daughter, *Anne*, became the wife of the Rev. John Cotton, A. M., of Hampton, N. H., by which marriage alone, it is believed Lake has any descendants in this country.

Mr. Cotton was son of the Rev. Seaboor Cotton, of Hampton, N. H., grandson of Rev. John Cotton, of Boston, and of Governor Simon Bradstreet; great grandson of Rev. Simon Bradstreet, of a wealthy Suffolk family, minister of Horbling, in Lincolnshire, sometime of Middleburg, in Holland, and of Hon. Thomas Dudley, first Deputy Governor, and third Governor, of Massachusetts. Mrs. Cotton, after the death of her husband, married the Rev. Increase Mather, D. D., of Boston. Her gravestone, in the ancient burial-place at Brookline, bears the following inscription: "Madam Anne Mather, relict of yᵉ Dr. Increase Mather, formerly wife of Revᵈ Mr. John Cotton; died at Brookline, March 29, 1737, Æ. s. 74." Sir Biby Lake, Baronet, son of Thomas of the Middle Temple, inherited the title and estate of his grand-uncle, Sir Edward.

The English branch has intermarried with the families of Winter, Crowther, Turner, King, Macbride, Webb, and others. Of this descent is Sir Willoughby Thomas Lake, K. C. B., Admiral of the White, in the British navy, Hon. Sir James Lake, Baronet, &c.

The New England branch has, in several generations, intermarried with the families of Gookin, Whiting, Upham, Thornton, Tracy, Lee, Wingate, Rogers, Jackson, Dearborn, Coffin, Hale, Storer, Bowles, Chadwick, &c.

JOHN MOUNTFORT. (p. 3.)

JOHN MOUNTFORT, founder of tomb No. 7, was brother to Jonathan Mountfort. They were the sons of Edmund Mountfort, who fled from England, in 1656, to Boston, in consequence of political offences, and who is referred to in "Dean & Smith's Journal," published in Portland, as an "educated merchant." In 1693, he married Mary Cock, granddaughter of Nicholas Upshall. In 1697 he was a member of the "Ancient and Honorable Artillery Company." He died, January 4, 1723. His descendants still reside in Boston, New York, and Louisiana.

MARY HART. (p. 13.)

MRS. HART, born at Lynn, 27th of May, 1699, was the daughter of Moses Hudson, (a descendant of Thomas Hudson, an ancient colonist at Lynn,) who, the "12th of November, 1685," married Sarah Collins, descended from "Henry Collins, of Lynn;" of whom Lewis, in his History of Lynn, says: He "embarked in the Abigail, of London, June 30, 1635; lands were granted to him in 1638; in 1639 he was a member of the Salem court; and in 1645, one of the selectmen of the town. He was born in 1606, and buried, February 20, 1687, at the age of eighty-one years. His wife, Ann, was born in 1605. His children were, Henry, born 1630; John, born 1632; Margery, born 1633; and Joseph, born 1635. He was associated with John Hathorne in 1662, in defending the town against a prosecution by William Longley. The first monthly meeting of Friends in Lynn was held at the house of Samuel Collins, July 18, 1690. There were only five Lynn men present."

Capt. Ralph Hart.

Capt. Hart was a well known and much-esteemed citizen of Boston. A copy of one of his commissions, following, is not without social and political interest, by contrast with the present time : —

Province of the }
Massachusetts=Bay. }

{ L. S. }

W I L L I A M   S H I R L E Y , Esq ;

Captain-General and GOVERNOUR in Chief, in and over His Majesty's Province of the *Massachusetts-Bay* in *New-England, &c.*

To Ralph Hart, *Gentleman, Greeting.*

BY virtue of the Power and Authority, in and by His Majesty's Royal Commission to Me granted, to be Captain-General, *&c.* over this His Majesty's Province of the *Massachusetts-Bay,* aforesaid ; I do (by these Presents) reposing especial Trust and Confidence in your Loyalty, Courage and good Conduct, constitute and appoint You the said Ralph Hart to be Lieutenant of the foot Company in the Town of Boston under the Command of Captⁿ Samuel Rand, in the Regiment of Militia, within the County of Suffolk, whereof Jacob Wendell Esq; is Colonel.

You are therefore carefully and diligently to discharge the Duty of a Lieutenant in leading, ordering and exercising said Company in Arms, both inferiour Officers and Soldiers, and to keep them in good Order and Discipline ; hereby commanding them to obey you as their Lieutenant, and your self to observe and follow such Orders and Instructions, as you shall from time to time receive from Me, or the Commander in Chief for the Time being, or other your Superiour Officers for His Majesty's Service, according to military Rules and Discipline, pursuant to the Trust reposed in you.

Given under My Hand & Seal at Arms, at Boston, the eleventh Day of February 3 o'clock, In the sixteenth Year of the Reign of His Majesty King GEORGE *the Second, Annoq; Domini,* 1742.

W. SHIRLEY.

By His Excellency's   Boston, Febry 28, 1742.
Command,
J. WILLARD, *Secry.*   *Sworn before*   JACOB WENDELL.
                                       WILLM. DOWNE.
                                       DAN. HENCHMAN.

In 1754, Lieut. Hart was Commissioned Captain of the Ancient and Honorable Artillery Company. His great grandfather, Samuel Hartt, born in England, about 1622, settled in Lynn, 1643–50, and was living in 1680, when his son, Samuel Hartt, Jun., was married, January 4, to Elizabeth Ingalls, a granddaughter of Mr. Edmund and Frances Ingalls, who came from Lincolnshire, in 1629, and were the first English people known to have been inhabitants of Lynn. Mrs. Hartt died, November 2, 1681, and he married his second wife, Abigail Lamberd, or Lambert, June 9, 1684. She was the daughter of Michael Lambert, who died at Lynn, August 18, 1676. Captain Ralph Hart, the son of the last marriage, was born at Lynn, the 12th of June, 1699. He married Mary Hudson, Nov. 27, 1722. Their daughter Mary was the wife of Mr. Joshua Bowles.

Joshua Bowles. (p. 11.)

Mr. Bowles, born at Roxbury, May 3, 1722, was a resident of the north end of Boston, and a deacon of the church there. He is described by one who remembers him, as of about five feet, eight inches in stature, of compact and muscular frame, and dark hair; as silent, and of reserved manners, "magnifying" his office in the church by a godly life and conversation, and honoring the precepts and examples of his fathers, particularly in the constant observance, during his life, of family devotions. He was brother-in-law to the Hon. Benjamin Lynde, of Salem, chief justice of the Province; and son of Major John Bowles, Esq., of Roxbury, by his wife, Lydia, daughter of Col. Samuel Checkley, Esq., of Boston, born at Preston Capes, in Northamptonshire, and sister of Rev. Samuel Checkley, of Boston.

Major Bowles was son of Hon. John Bowles, Esq., of Roxbury, by his wife, Sarah, daughter of the Rev. John Eliot, of Newton, and granddaughter of Rev. John Eliot, the "Apostle to the Indians." His son, Capt. Ralph Hart Bowles, served in the revolutionary army during the whole war of independence, and afterwards settled at Machias, Maine; where he held various civil offices, as clerk of the courts, justice of the peace, &c.* He married Hannah, daughter of Rev. Josiah Crocker, of Taunton, of the lineage of the Leonards, Cobbs, Thachers, Gorhams, Gov. Carver, Gov. Hinckley, and Hon. John Howland, of Plymouth.

Mrs. Bowles was distinguished for her energy of character, excellence of temper, and refinement of manners, peculiarly fitting her for usefulness in the frontier settlement at Machias. She died, July 10, 1847, aged 82, at Roxbury, and was interred at Mount Auburn, in the burial-place of her son, the late Stephen Jones Bowles.

Samuel Bowles, Esq., editor of the "Springfield Republican," is a descendant from Mr. Joshua Bowles.

* Born in Boston, March, 1759; died at Machias, Sept. 1813.

PARKMAN FAMILY. (pp. 27, 38.)

AN honored and distinguished branch of this family was Samuel Parkman, Esq., of whom, and of his father, the Rev. Ebenezer Parkman, of Westborough, Mass., we find the following notices in the Christian Examiner, of June, 1824 : —

"Died, in Boston, June 11, Samuel Parkman, Esq., aged seventy-two years ; one of the most distinguished and eminent merchants ; who raised himself to great opulence, without losing any thing of the moderation and simplicity of his original character and manners, or his strong attachment to the retired habits of domestic life. He was peculiarly domestic in his feelings, devoted to his family and friends, and singularly successful in the difficult duty of family government and discipline. Affectionate, yet firm, by judicious mixture of decision and kindness, he acquired, and maintained to the last, an unusually powerful influence with a numerous and most attached family. The loss of his counsels and affection is irreparable. He had been a professor of Christianity forty-three years, and deacon in the Second Church twenty-three years.* To the interests of that church he was zealously devoted, and gave frequent proofs of his attachment, which will long be remembered with gratitude. In his last disease, when informed that it must be fatal, he received the intelligence with

---

* Mr. Parkman was born Sept. 11, 1752. He was the son of Rev. Ebenezer Parkman, first minister of Westborough, Mass. ; who was graduated at Harvard College, in 1721 ; became a member of the New North Church in Boston, in 1723 ; was ordained in Westborough, then called Chauncy Village, in 1724 ; and after a faithful and devoted ministry of nearly sixty years, died Dec. 9, 1782, in the eightieth year of his age. He was honored among the most respectable clergymen of his day, devoting himself wholly to the duties of his calling. Besides some other publications, his Convention Sermon, preached in 1761, may be regarded as an honorable testimony of his enlightened and charitable, as well as fervent spirit.

perfect composure, and acquiesced without a murmur in the appointment of Heaven. Desirable as life continued to be, — and to few was it more so, — he surrendered it at once. He spoke with humility of his imperfections and unworthiness, and offered a fervent prayer that they might be forgiven, and that his attempts to do his duty might be accepted; declaring his trust to be in the mercy of God through Jesus Christ. His death was thus consistent with his profession, and brought consolation with it."

SARAH BROWN. (p. 53.)

MRS. BROWN, born at Ipswich, August 21, 1696, was daughter of Jonathan Cogswell, son of William, and grandson of John Cogswell, a London merchant, who settled in Ipswich, in 1635. Her mother (married, March 24, 1685) was daughter of Francis Wainwright, an eminent merchant of that town, and sister to Hon. John Wainwright. Miss Cogswell was married, in 1723, to Mr. James Brown, an opulent farmer of Ipswich, who died in the spring of 1741, leaving an estate of £6500. Mrs. Brown died in Boston, while visiting the family of her son-in-law, Mr. Timothy Thornton, (son of Ebenezer,) who, about 1773-4, moved to Ipswich, and there died, 4th September, 1787, aged sixty-one. The gravestone of her daughter, Eunice, at Ipswich, bears the following inscription: "Here lies what was mortal of Mrs. Eunice Thornton, wife of Mr. Timothy Thornton, who died Sept. 13th, 1784, in the 55th year of her age." They left two sons, viz.: Thomas Gilbert, the first son, born in Boston, August 31, 1768; married, November 26, 1793, Sarah, daughter to Hon. Thomas Cutts, of Saco, and died, March 24, 1824; their son, J. B. Thornton, married Eliza, daughter of Hon. Daniel Gookin, of Northampton, N. H.; and daughter, Anna Paine, married Gov. John Fairfield, of Saco, late United States Senator from Maine. James Brown, the second son, married Ruth, daughter of Mr. Samuel Sewall, of York, county of York, and died, in 1825, without issue.

TIMOTHY THORNTON. (p. 56.)

MR. THORNTON was the son of the Rev. Thomas Thornton, of Yarmouth, Mass. He was born about 1647 : a principal citizen of Boston, where he was admitted a freeman, May 15, 1672. He was several times chosen one of the " Commissioners " of Boston — a court of record created by the Acts of 1651 and 1654. Says Judge Sewall, date April 4, 1690, " This day, Capt. Theophilus Frary, Adam Winthrop, Mr. Jno. Clark, Timo. Thornton," and others, " are chosen Commissioners for yᵉ town of Boston." December 17th, 1690, Mr. Thornton, Major Elisha Hutchinson, Major John Phillips, Capt. Penn Townsend, and Mr. Adam Winthrop, were appointed by the Legislature a committee to issue bills of credit to pay the debts of the recent French and Indian wars. This was the first paper currency in Massachusetts. Mr. Thornton was several times elected " selectman " of Boston; in 1693, he, with Ephraim Savage, Samuel Checkley, and Edward Bromfield, were chosen. In 1693, Mr. Thornton, Penn Townsend, and Edward Bromfield, were chosen Representatives from Boston. Mr. Thornton was a Representative in 1694 and 1695.

Judge Sewall wrote in his journal, " 1714-5, January 10th, snowy day. Mr. Gee sends his son to invite me to Dinner tomorrow at his house." " Tuesday, January 11th, went thither, where din'd Dr. Incr. & Dr. C. Mather, Mr. Bridge, Mr. Wadsworth, Mr. Thornton, Mr. Jno. Marion, Deacon Barnard, Mr. Ruck, Capt. Martyn, Mr. Hallowell. It seems it was in remembrance of his landing this day at Boston after his Algerine captivity. Had a good Treat. Dr. Cotton Mather, in returning Thanks, very well comprised many weighty things very pertinently." "1714–5, Feb. 2d, Went to yᵉ Meeting at Broʳ Thornton's; read out of Mr. Shepard on the Virgins — *They yᵗ were ready went in.* Sung clauses out of yᵉ 45th Psalm."

All his children were by his first wife, Experience, who died March 23, 1694. They were Mary, born 1674, April 2; Thomas; Elizabeth, b. Nov. 17, 1677, m. Major Thomas Wade, Esq., April 4, 1700; Ann; Timothy, b. May 6, 1681; Catharine, b. April 16, 1683, m. Isaac Russel, of Boston; Experience, b. Feb. 23, 1687, m. Jonathan Coolidge, of Watertown; Ebenezer, baptized by Dr. Mather, Jan. 12, 1690, m. Elizabeth, daughter of Capt. Thomas Gilbert, of Boston; died in Watertown, about 1749. The following inscription is from the gravestone of his wife, in the ancient burial-ground at Watertown: "Mrs. Elizabeth Thornton, who departed this life June 10th, 1740, Æt. 37 years."

Mrs. SARAH THORNTON was the second wife, and widow of Mr. Timothy Thornton, of Boston. Her name before marriage is unknown.

JONATHAN MOUNTFORT. (p. 81.)

JONATHAN MOUNTFORT, founder of tomb 59, brother of John, was a man of liberal education, a physician and apothecary, and resided for many years at what was called "Mountfort's Corner." He was independent in his means, and eccentric in his habits. In 1719, he was one of the seceders from the New North Church, and among the founders and building committee of the "New Brick," or "*weathercock*" church, for whom he was treasurer. His descendants in the male line are extinct; in the female line, they are merged with the Greenough and Pitts families.

The Mountfort family coat of arms, as represented over the tomb of Jonathan Mountfort, belonged to Hugo de Montfort, a Norman, who, in 1066, commanded the cavalry of William the Conqueror at the battle of Hastings.

This name is known in the "History of England," during the reigns of William I., Henry II., Henry III., John, Edward I., Edward III., Edward IV., and Henry VII. It is especially referred to in "Dugdale's History of Warwickshire," a copy of which is in the library of Harvard University, which represents the same coat of arms as those over the tomb, and gives an elaborate and authentic pedigree of the family, from Turstain de Montfort, 1030, father of Hugo, as above mentioned, to Simon Mountfort, 1633, father of Edmund, and grandfather of John and Jonathan Mountfort, founders of tombs Nos. 7 and 59.

It is also referred to in "Collin's Peerage," "Burke's Extinct Peerage," "Wiffan's History of the House of Russell," and other works.

GRANT FAMILY. (p. 107.)

THE space enclosed within an iron railing near the centre of the cemetery, and which contains the tomb of the Grant family, was not originally a part of the cemetery. This small canton of land was purchased by the first proprietor, [see deed below,] Mr. Gee, of the owner of a field adjoining the cemetery, his lady wishing to have a last resting-place apart from the multitude. It became the property of the Grant family, by purchase, four generations back, and is now owned by Deacon Moses Grant, to whom the interest in it of the other heirs of his father, the late Deacon Moses Grant, was conveyed, on his decease. The property being, as has been remarked, held in fee, and under no restraint as to its use, a dwelling-house, or any other structure, could be erected on the spot; and, what is more, the proprietor has a right of way over the cemetery, which right of way is by common law construed to mean a path broad enough for cart wheels to pass over. We need not, however, apprehend that the worthy proprietor or any of his descendants will avail themselves of their private rights, to the inconvenience of the public.

This enclosure holds the remains of three generations of the Grant family. Moses Grant, Esq., who was buried here in 1817, aged seventy-three, was deacon of Brattle Street Church; and Samuel Grant, Esq., who was buried in 1784, aged eighty, was deacon of the old North Church, (Dr. Andrew Eliot's.)

The late respected Deacon Moses Grant was in revolutionary times a very ardent patriot. He was one of the *destroyers of the tea*, and one of the party who were engaged in the bold and successful attempt to remove the two pieces of cannon by night to the American lines, and who narrowly escaped the pursuit of the British guard.

One of our elder citizens remembers seeing a London newspaper of 1774, which contained a letter from Boston, written during the troubles, and referring to some of the principal actors. It had this passage: "There is *Deacon* Grant, a member of the *Cadet Company* — a fiery *deacon* indeed!" The patriotic composition of that company, at the time of these events, may be inferred from the fact that its commander was Colonel John Hancock!

—

To all Christian People to whom this present Deed of Sale Shall Come, Samuel Sewall of Boston in the County of Suffolk in the Province of the Massachusetts Bay in New England Esqr and Hannah his Wife send Greeting. Now Know ye that the said Sam¹ Sewall and Hannah his Wife for divers good

Considerations, and especially in Consideration of Two and
Thirty Shillings paid them, Have Given, sold, aliened, enfeoffed
and confirmed, And by these Presents Do Give Sell, aliene
enfeoff and confirm unto Joshua Gee of the said Boston Ship-
wright, One Rod square of Land in the said Boston, being
part of their pasture at the North-End adjoining to the North-
burying place, in which parcel of Ground Mrs Mary Thacher
now lyeth buried, bounded Northerly by the said Burying-
Place, and on all other sides by the Land of the said Samuel
& Hannah Sewall. TO HAVE and TO HOLD the above
granted Rod of Ground to him the said Joshua Gee and his
Heirs for Ever. And it is to be understood that the said
Joshua Gee is to have No Way to the above granted Land but
what he has through the North-burying place. And the said
Joshua Gee is to make and maintain all the Fence, except one
half Rod of the Southerly part of the Granted Land. In
Witness whereof the sd Samuel Sewall and Hannah his Wife
have hereunto set their Hands and Seals this Seventh day of
January, 170$\frac{8}{9}$ Annoque Regni Annæ Magnæ Britaniæ &c.
Reginæ, Septimo.

SAMUEL SEWALL [L. S.]
HANNAH SEWALL [L. S.]

Signed Seal'd and Deliver'd In presence of
MARY SEWALL
DAVID SINCLAR

Suffolk Ss   The Within named Samuel Sewall and Hannah His Wife Personally Appearing before me the Subscrib[r]
One of Her Majesty's Justices of the Peace for the County
afores[d] Acknowledged the within written Instrument to be their
Act and Deed this 20th of Jan. 170$\frac{8}{9}$

EDMUND QUINSEY, *J. Peace*

Boston January the 20th 1710
Received and Recorded with the Records of Deeds for the
County of Suffolk Libo XXV to fol 174 &c.

ADDINGTON DAVENPORT *Regist'r*

[THERE are more inscriptions bearing the name of "SNELLING" than any other in this cemetery, and I have been very desirous of obtaining some account of the history of this family. All the information that I have as yet been able to obtain is contained in the pedigree given below.]

PEDIGREE OF SNELLING.

Willms Snelling de Chetlewood in Com. Deuon. ==Jana filia Edm : Speccott de Thoruerton in Deuon.

Thomas Snelling de Chadlewood in Com. Deuon superstes 1620. ==Johanna filia et hær Elford de Comitatu Deuoniæ.

Florence 3. filia uxor ... Supp.

Welthian 2. filia Nupta Furse de Com. Deuoniæ.

Johanna uxor .... Broken de Plimouth in Comitat Deuon.

Maria Nupta .... Martin de Plimouth.

5. Johanna.
6. Dorothea.

3. Emanuell.
4. Willmus.

Johannes Snelling de Chadlewood in Comitat Deuon superstes 1620. ==Francisca filia Walton Hele. de Gnaton in Com. Deuon ao.

Thomas Snelling, 2. filius.

Elizabeth. Maria. Twinnes.

3. Francisca.
4. Johanna.
5. Jana.

Anna. filia. 6.

Georgius Snelling filius et hæres ætatis 10 annorum 1620.
2. Samson.
3. Johannes.*

I do hereby certify the above to be faithfully copied from the Visitation Book of the County of Devon, ao. 1620, now in the College of Arms, London, this 26th June, 1841.

THOS. WM. KING, Rougedragon.

* Father of Thomas, who emigrated to America, and ancestor of the American branch of this family.

Mariners' Receiving Tomb. (p. 128.)

The Mariners' Monumental Receiving Tomb, in Copp's Hill Cemetery, Boston, was procured by contributions from seamen and their friends.

The noble crew of the U. S. sloop-of-war Albany presented Phineas Stow, pastor of the Baptist Bethel, Boston, with fifty-two dollars, for this worthy object; and Martin Woodworth, a generous sailor, collected three hundred dollars from the merchants in a few days. The enterprise met with their cordial approval.

It may not be improper to state, that many seamen who have been found dead in the docks, or have been accidentally (as we say) killed by falling from the yard-arm of a ship, have been buried by the city without any religious services whatever. We would cast no reflections upon the worthy citizens of Boston; for in the arrangements of the city for burying the poor, seamen have shared, as well as others who have died away from home and kindred. The writer, to give mariners a more appropriate burial, has procured from Coroners Pratt and Smith the remains of seamen, and incurred expenses, which have been cheerfully paid by seamen and others. Public attention has been called to the proper interment of sailors, and the call has been nobly responded to. The writer's father was a sea captain, his only brother is also a shipmaster, and his relatives are engaged in navigating the ocean. It is natural that tender emotions should be awakened in his bosom for the stranger who finds an early grave far from his native home.

The smiles of an approving Heaven have attended this work of humanity. It has called into exercise the better feelings and sympathies of those who are directly engaged in a business, the tendency of which is to shorten human life. It is cheering that, in this world of strife and tumult, there is a common ground on which all may stand.

Beautiful shells are to be cemented on the shaft of this monument. Many sailors and their friends have given moaning ocean shells, which may sing a requiem over the sailor's resting-place.

The disciples of John the Baptist "came and took up his corpse, and laid it in a tomb." (Mark vi. 29.) So we wish to lay in a tomb the mortal remains of the toil-worn sailor, who often dies homeless, friendless, and penniless. Seamen should have a "memorial" in the city of Boston — a city which has been enriched by commerce — the fruits of the toil and sufferings of mariners. Boston will not wrong the *ocean children.* The proprietor of the Woodland Cemetery, in Malden, has kindly given a large lot, where the bodies can be deposited when the receiving tomb shall be full. A monument will be erected there in memory of seamen.

The first three bodies deposited in the Mariners' Tomb belonged to three different nations — England, Sweden, and America — and occupied three different positions in the service — captain, officer, and sailor, — but no distinctions are known there; they rest peacefully side by side.

"It is their watch below."

A female, a true friend of seamen, was the fourth body deposited in the tomb. Three days before her death, she saw the monument that was to be erected on this tomb. It was completed the very day she was struck with death. Her husband was called upon by a gentleman to go and see the monument, when he informed his friend that his wife was dying. It was like an electric shock. The history of this tomb is thus mournfully interesting to him, who, with his departed companion, for years devoted himself to benefit the long-neglected sailor.

The reflex influence of efforts to respect and benefit humanity will not fail to bless the living. The author of this work has generously given ten copies of the book to the sailor's cause. By his request, the writer of the above has given the foregoing particulars, which may not be devoid of interest. Mr. Bridgman's work will meet with the sympathy and approbation of all who are connected by ties of kindred and affection with the sleeping denizens of Copp's Hill Burying-ground. "The memory of the *just* is blessed." (Prov. x. 7.)

GREENWOOD. (p. 14.)

ISAAC GREENWOOD ; graduated at Harvard College, in 1721 ; chosen Hollis Professor of Mathematics and Natural Philosophy of that institution, May 12th, 1727 ; died in 1745.

Rev. Francis W. P. Greenwood, D. D. ; born Feb. 5th, 1797 ; graduated at Harvard College, in 1814 ; died August 2d, 1843.

William Pitt Greenwood ; born May 10th, 1766 ; died May 10th, 1851, on his eighty-fifth birthday.

REV. THOMAS THORNTON. (p. 162.)

THE Rev. Thomas Thornton was one of the noble company of Nonconformists who were ejected or silenced by the Act of Uniformity, St. Bartholomew's Day, August 24, 1662. — *Mather's Magnalia*, Book III. fol. 4. He was the successor of the Rev. John Miller, and third pastor of the church in Yarmouth, from about 1663 to the autumn of 1693, or spring of 1694, when he removed to Boston, and resided with his children during the remainder of his life, his son, Timothy, contributing liberally for his support and comfort in his declining years. In 1691, the Rev. John Cotton was associated with him in the ministry, to relieve him from the cares too heavy for his advanced age; and after his removal to Boston, his people still cheered him with frequent tokens of affectionate remembrance. His fellow-sufferer under the Act of Uniformity, the Rev. Thomas Walley, for a while lived in Yarmouth, but was soon settled in the ministry, at Barnstable, the adjacent town.

A glimpse at Mr. Thornton's life in Boston, and an interesting exhibition of the character and habits of our great and good men of ancient times, occur in the following extract from the diary of Chief Justice Samuel Sewall: "Aug. 13, 1695. We have a fast Kept in our *new* chamber. Mr. Willard begins wth prayer and preaches from 2^d Chronicles, xxxiv. 27. Mr. Allen prays." "P. M. Mr. Bayly begins with prayer, preaches from Luke i. 50, and then concludes with prayer. Sung ye 27 Ps. 7–10, [the version in use was the New England Psalm-book.] I set Windsor tune, and burst so into tears y^t I could scarce continue singing. Mr. Thornton was here, but went away when Mr. Allen was at Prayer. Mr. Cook and Mr. Addington here. Mr. Serg^t was diverted," &c. "I appointed y^s day to ask God's Blessing after ye death of my dear mother, and in particular to bless Sam. wth a Master & calling, and bless us in our *new* house. The Lord pardon and doe for us beyond our hopes contrary to our Deserts."

Judge Sewall visited Mr. Thornton during his last illness, and recorded minutely the incidents of his sickness and death. " Feb. 15, 3 p. m. Mr. Tho: Thornton dies very quietly, wch Mr. Gee acquaints me wth. Is very near 93 years old."

He was born in 1609, the son of John Thornton, of Bidforth, in Yorkshire, born in 1581, living 1612, and grandson of Thomas Thornton, by Helen, daughter to Percival, son to the Lord Lumley. His mother was Grace, daughter of Thomas Wythers, of Copgrave.* The Christian merchants, Henry Thornton and John Thornton, of England, were of the same family.

Mr. Thornton's children were, Mary, who married Judah,

* Herald's Visitations, Yorkshire, 1530, 1584, 1612.

son of Rev. Mr. Anthony Thacher, brother of Rev. Peter Thacher, Rector of St. Edmunds, in Salisbury, in England, for nineteen years; Elizabeth, who married Mr. Joshua Gee, of Boston, and afterwards the Rev. Peter Thacher, of Milton; Thomas; Anna, married to Dr. Nathaniel Hall, of Yarmouth, and afterwards of Hingham; Theophilus; TIMOTHY, who married Experience ———, and Priscilla, of whom Mather gives an account in his *Magnalia.*

NICHOLAS UPSHALL. (p. 187.)

NICHOLAS UPSHALL was the twenty-third member on the roll of the " Ancient and Honorable Artillery Company." In 1637, he owned property from Hanover Street to the water, on the north-east side of Richmond Street, which was laid out in 1636. He left his property to his two daughters — wife of William Greenough, and the wife of Joseph Cock. He was grandfather to the wife of John Mountfort, founder of tomb No. 7. He was fined £20, and exiled by the government of " Massachusetts colony," for bribing the keeper of Boston jail to supply two Quaker women, then in prison, with food, otherwise they would have starved to death; and afterwards, for expressing his abhorrence in relation to the inhuman and tyrannous acts of Governor Endicott and others towards the Quakers, — although he was of much influence, property, &c., and also a member of the church, — he was banished the colony, and resided six years in Rhode Island. On his return, he furnished a room in his house for the free use of the Quakers. The " History of the Ancient and Honorable Artillery Company " says, in reference to Nicholas Upshall, " Property, moral worth, public services, wife, children, friends, cannot preserve a man from the ruthless fangs of religious persecution. The respectable Quakers of the present day, (Lynn,) have recently reclaimed the remains of their former brethren from the old Quaker burial-ground, lest the rapacious hands of speculation should trespass further. Why do they not redeem the ashes of those who may be considered among the first martyrs of their sect?"

ELEAZER PRATT.

ELEAZER PRATT (interred in the tomb of Eliot, Kimball, and Pratt) was a lineal descendant from Phinehas Pratt, one of the first planters of New England. He was born in Cohasset, and came to Boston at about the age of sixteen years. He resided here until the day of his death, August 21, 1849, when he died with the Asiatic cholera, at the age of sixty-four years and seven months.

Nature endowed him with a remarkable constitution. Previous to his death, he was never but once obliged to call for a physician, and his prospect for a long life to come was very promising — his ancestors, and his seven brothers and sisters having attained an age far beyond his; the brothers and sisters now remaining very hale, at an average age of seventy-seven years.

With a good constitution, he also possessed a sound mind, which he constantly exercised in the study of mankind. He died in the full belief, that when his earthly tabernacle was dissolved, he should have a building of God, eternal in the heavens.

Eleazer Pratt's sister, Abigail, is now eighty years of age; she never took any medicine. Last winter, she walked from Boston to Somerville, a distance of four miles, without much fatigue. His brother, Benjamin, aged upwards of eighty-two years, went into the woods last winter, and assisted in cutting his supply of wood for the season.

LORING, CUSHING, SPEAR, AND GRAY,

DESCENDANTS of Deacon Thomas Loring, and his wife, Jane Newton, who came from Axminster, Devonshire, England, Dec. 22, 1634, with their two sons, and settled at Hingham, New England, in 1635. From the "Ancestral Records of the Loring Family of Massachusetts Bay. In four parts. Exhibiting the Genealogy of the four sons of Deacon Thomas Loring, extending through seven generations. By James S. Loring."

1. THOMAS, born in 1629; married Hannah, daughter of Nicholas Jacob, of Hingham, Dec. 13, 1657. Their children were, Hannah, born Aug. 9, 1664, who married Rev. Jeremiah Cushing, of Scituate, in 1685. Thomas, born July 29, 1667; married Deborah, daughter of Hon. John Cushing, of Scituate, April 19, 1699. Deborah, born March 15, 1668; married Hon. John Cushing, of Scituate, June 20, 1688. David, born Sept. 15, 1671; married Elizabeth, daughter of Hon. John Otis, of

Barnstable, Jan. 1699. Caleb, born June 9, 1674; married Lydia, daughter of Edward Gray of Plymouth, Aug. 7, 1696.

2. JOHN, born Dec. 22, 1630; married Mary, daughter of Nathaniel Baker, of Hingham, Dec. 16, 1657; and married second time widow Rachel Buckland, Sept. 22, 1679. Their children were, John, born in 1658, who died in 1678. Joseph, born March 10, 1660; married Hannah, daughter of John Leavitt, Oct. 25, 1683. Thomas, born March 1, 1662; married Leah, daughter of Benjamin Buckland, Jan. 10, 1687. Sarah, born, 1664, died early. Isaac, born Jan. 22, 1666; married Sarah Young, Aug. 5, 1691, of Boston. Mary, born Feb., 1668; married Thomas Jones, of Hull. Nathaniel, born March 5, 1670; married Susanna Butler, of Boston, Dec. 13, 1699. Daniel, born Feb. 8, 1672; married Priscilla Mann, of Boston, Feb. 2, 1698. Rachel, born Feb. 29, 1674; married Caleb Hobart, Sept. 23, 1700. Jacob, born April 21, 1676; married Sarah Lewis, Feb. 9, 1709. Israel, born 1678, died same year. John, born June 20, 1680; married Jane, daughter of Samuel Baker, Sept. 2, 1703. Israel, born April 15, 1682; married Mary, daughter of Nathan Hayman, of Charlestown, May 25, 1709. Sarah, born June 6, 1684. Caleb, born Jan. 2, 1689; married Elizabeth Baker, June 22, 1714.

3. JOSIAH, born in 1637; and married Elizabeth Prince, daughter of Elder John Prince, of Hull. Their children were, Jane, born Aug. 9, 1663; married Samuel Gifford, of Sandwich. Josiah, born Nov. 22, 1665. Samuel, born 1668, died 1674. Jonathan, born April 24, 1674; married Elizabeth, daughter of Richard Austin, of Charlestown. Job, born Feb. 22, 1669; married Rebecca, name not known, and settled at Rochester, Mass. Elizabeth, born 1672; died 1743.

4. BENJAMIN, baptized Jan. 9, 1642; married Mary, daughter of Matthew Hawke, of Hingham, Dec. 8, 1670. Their children were, Benjamin, born 1671, who married Anna, daughter of Isaac Vickory, Oct. 8, 1702. John, born about 1673; married Elizabeth, daughter of John Collier, Feb. 10, 1709. Mary, born 1675; married James Gould, Feb. 8, 1709.

Samuel, born 1680; married Jane, daughter of John Collier, April 19, 1716. Matthew, born Oct. 19, 1684; married Experience, daughter of John Collier, Dec. 23, 1714.

The decease of the common ancestor is thus recorded in Hobart's Diary : "1661, April 1. Thomas Loring, sometime a deacon to the church at Hingham, died at Hull." His widow, Jane, had the improvement of the estate until her decease, Aug. 25, 1672. By her will, dated July 10, 1672, she appointed her son Thomas executor. Among other legacies, she bequeathed to her son Thomas a volume called "The Jewell of Contentment, by Jeremiah Burroughs. Printed at London, in 1645." To Hannah, wife of Thomas, a yellow pair of bodices, stomacher, her best neck clothes, &c.; to her son, John, a volume called "The Covenant of Grace, by Obadiah Sedgwick." To Mary, wife of John, a suit of head linen, her best mantle, a kersey waistcoat with gold lace, and other articles; to her son Benjamin, a volume called "The True, or Sincere Convert, by Thomas Sheppard, of London, discovering the small number of true Beleevers, and the Great Difficulty of Saving Conversion." Also her interest in a "Catch," or vessel at sea. To Mary, wife of Benjamin, her riding suit, pillion cloth, hood and gloves, a suit of head clothes, serge gown, and other articles. To her son Josiah she gave twenty pounds of wool, to clothe his children. Rev. Zechariah Whitman was a witness to the will; proved, Boston, Oct. 6, 1672. The agreement of the four sons of Deacon Thomas Loring, in the division of their father's estate, Oct. 30, 1672, is in the probate office of Suffolk.

Heraldry. — Arms of Sir Petrus Loring, granted in the reign of Henry III.: Shield — quarterly, argent and gules, a bend engrailed, sable, for Loring. Crest — five upright feathers, standing in a bowl, argent.

From "Memorials of the Cushing Family, of Hingham and Scituate, New England, descendants of Daniel Cushing, Esq., and Hon. John Cushing, sons of Deacon Matthew Cushing, of

Hingham, Norfolk County, Old England, in 1638. By J. S.
Loring."

Peter Cushing, of Hingham, Norfolk county, England, who,
according to Deane, held large estates in Lombard Street,
London, had two sons, Theophilus and Matthew, who came to
New England. The former, born in 1579, sailed in the ship
Griffin, in 1633, in company with Governor Haynes; resided
on his farm, and finally settled in Hingham. He was blind for
twenty-five years, had no family, and died March 24, 1678.
The younger son, Matthew, born in 1588, married Nazareth,
daughter of Henry Pitcher, Aug. 5, 1613, and had four sons,
and one daughter, who married Matthias Briggs, May, 1648;
all natives of Hingham, Old England. He embarked with his
whole family and his wife's sister, widow Frances Riecroft, in
the ship Diligent, of Ipswich, three hundred and fifty tons,
John Martin, master; arrived at Boston, Aug. 10, 1638, with
one hundred and thirty-three passengers, among whom was
Robert Peck, teacher, and settled at Hingham, in that year,
where he had a grant of land, and became a deacon of Rev.
Peter Hobart's church. He died Sept. 30, 1660, leaving a will.
His widow died Jan. 6, 1691, aged ninety-five years. But two
of his sons left descendants, Daniel and John, the former of
whom was a justice of the peace, and the third town clerk of
Hingham.

1. DANIEL, married Lydia, daughter of Edward Gilman,
Jan, 19, 1645. Their children were, Peter, born 1646, who
married Hannah Hawke, 1685. Daniel, born 1648, who married Elizabeth Thaxter, in 1680. Deborah, born in 1651, who
married Benjamin Woodbridge, 1679. Jeremiah, born in 1654,
who married Hannah Loring, in 1685. Theophilus, born in
1657, who married Mary Thaxter, in 1688. Matthew, born in
1660, who married Jael Jacob, in 1684.

Daniel Cushing, Esq., died Dec. 3, 1700.

2. Hon. JOHN, married Sarah, daughter of Matthew Hawke.
Their children were, John, born in 1662, who married Deborah
Loring, in 1688. Thomas, born in 1663, who married Deborah

Thaxter, in 1687. Matthew, born in 1664, who married Deborah Jacob, in 1689. Jeremiah, born in 1666, who married Judith Parmenter, in 1693. James, born in 1668, who married Mary Barrell, in 1712. Joshua, born in 1670. Sarah, born in 1671, who married Dea. David Jacob, in 1689. Caleb, born Jan. 6, 1672, who married Elizabeth Cotton, in 1698. Mary, born 1676, died 1698. Deborah, born 1674; married Thomas Loring, 1699. Joseph, born in 1677; married Mercy Pickles, in 1710. Benjamin, born in 1678; became a merchant of Barbadoes.

The arms of the Cushing Family are quarterly, gu. an eagle, argent. Gules, three right hands somewhat torn. A canton chequery or. and az. 1563.

DESCENDANTS OF GEORGE SPEAR. He was an early inhabitant of Dorchester, and was admitted freeman in 1644. He soon removed to Braintree, now Quincy, where he died. His wife's name was Mary, who died Dec. 7, 1674. He was probably the ancestor of all of the name in New England. Their children were, George, who married Mary Deerings, 1669. Sarah, born 1647; married George Witly, 1672. Samuel, born 1659; married Elizabeth Daniels, 1694. Ebenezer, born 1654. Richard. Hannah, married Simeon Bryant, 1694. Nathaniel, born 1665; married Hannah Holman, 1689.

1. SAMUEL, son of George, lived near Horse Neck, where he died, 1713, before the birth of his youngest child. He has a gravestone in Quincy. His estate, appraised 1714, at £111,810. He had Samuel, 1696; graduated at Harvard University, 1715; married Rebecca Hinckley. He had the "Great Hill," which, with what was bestowed in his education, was a double portion; also forty acres, the part of his sister, Hannah Lemont, which he bought of her. Daniel, born 1698; probably died young. Elizabeth, born 1700; died 1724. Mehitabel, born 1702; married Benjamin Neal, 1727. Dorothy, married Benjamin Veazie, 1726. Hannah, born 1706; married Robert Lemont, 1729. William, born 1708; married Hannah

Penniman, 1730. He had the dwelling-house lately occupied by Joseph Green, and about sixteen acres of land on the site ; also two acres in Penniman's Meadow, and ten acres in Mills's Meadow. John, born 1710 ; married Mary Arnold, 1736. He had the dwelling-house lately occupied by Mr. Nightingale, barn, and two acres of woodland. Mary, born 1712 ; married John Saunders, 1735. She had twenty-six acres of land at Horse Neck. Benoni, born 1714 ; married Elizabeth Newcomb, 1760. He had twenty-seven acres of his father's land. John Spear's daughter Prudence, born 1737, married Daniel Baxter, in 1755.

2. GEORGE, son of George 1st, married Mary Deerings. She died 1678. They had Mary, 1676. Ebenezer, 1678, who died same year.

3. EBENEZER, son of George 1st, married Rachel Deerings, 1679, and lived in Braintree. They were members of the church in the south parish, in 1711, and many of their descendants have lived there. He died, March, 1719. They had Ebenezer, 1680, who married Mary Copeland, 1718, and second wife, Mary Tower, 1727. Mary, born 1682 ; married Ephraim Jones, 1708. Samuel, born 1684, who married Rebecca. Rachel, born 1686 ; married Cornelius Thayer, of Braintree, 1717. Joseph, born Feb. 25, 1688 ; married Ann. She died, April, 1719. He married second wife, Mary Collier, of Hull, Dec. 12, 1720. He was ancestor of the Spears of Hull. Nathaniel, born 1693. Abigail, born 1695 ; married Nathaniel Littlefield, 1718. Benjamin, born 1698 ; married Sarah Niles, 1722. Deering, born 1700 ; married Jemima Thayer, 1726. Son Nathaniel, administrator.

4. RICHARD, son of George 1st, married, and had seven children, all of whom were baptized, April 11, 1698, in Braintree, viz.: Rebecca, Benjamin, Richard, John, James, Mary, and Deborah.

5. NATHANIEL, son of George 1st, married Hannah Holman, 1689, and lived in Braintree, where he died, leaving a will, Sept. 12, 1728. His wife died, 1725. Their children were,

Hannah, born 1690, who married Ebenezer Nightingale, 1711. Nathaniel, born 1692; married Thankful. John, born 1694; married Ann Perry, of Milton, 1718. Mary, born 1697; married Lemuel Gulliver, 1717. David, born 1699; married Deborah. Joseph, born 1701; married Abigail Cleg. Nathan, born 1703; married Mehitabel Brackett, 1734. Margaret, born 1710. Thomas, born 1707; died young. Lydia, born 1713; married Richard Bracket, 1733.

THE GRAY FAMILY, OF BOSTON. Edward Gray, an opulent merchant of Boston, arrived in this country, from Lancashire, England, in 1686. He served an apprenticeship with Mr. Barton, as a ropemaker, at Barton's Point, then a cow pasture. He hired Barton's Point and ropewalk of Mr. Barton, for ten dollars per annum. He was married to Susanna Harrison, by Pen Townsend, Esq., 1699; had Harrison, 1711; who married Elizabeth Lewis, 1734. Treasurer of Massachusetts Province, and left Boston with the British troops in 1776, as did his grandson Harrison, who died at London, 1830, aged ninety. Harrison senior had also, John, born 1755. Lewis. Elizabeth, 1746; married Samuel A. Otis, father of Hon. H. G. Otis. Edward senior had Edward, 1702; married Hannah Bridge, 1727; had Edward, 1728. Sarah, married Jeremy Green. Anne, born 1705; married Increase Blake. Persis, born 1706. Bethiah, born 1710. Susannah, born 1712; married Col. Joseph Jackson. John, born 1713; married Mary Otis, Barnstable. His second wife was Hannah Ellis, married by Dr. Colman, 1714; a niece of Dr. Colman's wife, who sent for her from England, with a view to this marriage, owing to her warm affection called the *lump of love;* and had Ellis, 1716; married Sarah Tyler, by Rev. William Welsted, 1739. Ellis was colleague pastor of Second Church, Boston; had Hannah, 1744; married Thomas Cary, late of Chelsea, one of whose daughters was wife of Rev. Dr. Tuckerman. He had also, Ellis, 1745. William, born 1747. Mary, daughter of Edward, senior, married Nathaniel Loring, 1739, a grandson of Elder

John Loring, of Hull. Also, William, 1724; married Elizabeth Hall, daughter of Capt. Stephen Hall. Benjamin, born 1726; married Mary Blanchard. Thomas, a bachelor. Judge Hall, of Boston, married Sarah, daughter of Ellis Gray, Jr. Judge Wilson, of Washington, and Dr. Bartlett, Boston, married Hannah, daughter of Ellis Gray, Jr. Edward, senior, died 1757, aged eighty-four. Dr. Chauncy said of him, in a funeral sermon, "He was unexceptionable, unenvied, except for his goodness, universally well spoken of, both while living and now he is dead." By his will, dated Feb. 12, 1753, (witnessed by James Otis, the patriot,) Mr. Gray gave to his son John the ropewalks, seven hundred and forty-four feet in length, by twenty or more feet wide, a brick warehouse adjoining, with yarn-house, knotting-house, dwelling-house, and land, standing the whole length of the present Pearl Street, and on Cow Lane, now High Street and Atkinson Street, appraised at one thousand pounds. The whole estate was appraised at about £5500. By the inventory, he had ten colored slaves, appraised at about £246.

William Gray, son of Edward, senior, had Martha Hall, 1760; married Dr. Samuel Danforth. Stephen H., born 1761. William, born 1762. Edward, born 1764; married Susanna Turell, who had John. Rev. Frederick Turell, who married Elizabeth P. Chapman, and had also two daughters. John, born 1768. Elizabeth Saunders, born 1769; married Jacob Eustis. Rev Dr. Thomas, of Jamaica Plain, born 1772; married Deborah, daughter of Rev. Dr. Samuel Stillman, 1793; had George Harrison, 1795; married Ann, daughter of Dr. Terence Wakefield. Hannah Stillman, born 1796. Ann Greenough, born 1800; married Rev. George Whitney. Thomas, born 1806, who was a physician and a poet.

Hiram Smith. (p. 197.)

These infant children of Hiram and Sarah Smith were buried in the family vault, No. 98. Their remains have been removed to Mr. Smith's tomb, in Moss Path, Mount Auburn Cemetery. The record is from a mourning piece, wrought in childhood, by the eldest surviving daughter.

The other children of Mr. Smith are now living : Sarah Eliza, wife of Dr. Nathaniel B. Shurtleff, of Boston; Maria Augusta S. Smith; Caroline H., wife of Perez B. Howard, of Wareham; and Almira P., wife of Wesley P. Balch, of Boston.

Sigourney. (p. 137.)

The name of Sigourney is found among that band of Huguenots who sought refuge in New England from the persecutions that succeeded the revocation of the edict of Nantes by Louis XIV. The ancestor of the American branch of that family, Andrew Sigourney, or, according to the French orthography, Andrè Sejournè, came to Boston, with other emigrants, in the winter of 1686, and died in that city, in 1727, at the age of eighty-eight. He brought with him his son Andrew, a boy of thirteen, who married Mary Germaine, in 1696, and died in Boston, at the age of seventy-five.

The Sigourneys belonged to those exiles from France, who, with their pastor, Pierre Daillè, formed a settlement at Oxford, in Worcester county, on the banks of a stream which still retains the appellation they gave it, of French River. The vestiges of a fort erected by them, on a commanding height, are distinctly visible. In consequence of an inroad and massacre by a neighboring tribe of Indians, they relinquished their colonial establishment, and returned to Boston about the year

1700, where they and their descendants have become incorporated among its most worthy and respected inhabitants.

The pastor, Daillè, beloved almost to adoration by his peaceful and pious flock, died in 1715. Two lowly graves in the Granary burying-ground bear the inscription of the "Reverend Pierre Daillè," and "Seyre, his wife." He was succeeded in his sacred office by the Rev. Andrew Le Mercier, author of an ecclesiastical history of Geneva. The earliest place of worship of this interesting people occupied the site of the present Universalist meeting-house in School Street, and is designated in the records of those times, as the "French Protestant Church." These, like other Huguenots who took refuge in different parts of our country from the persecution of a tyrant king, by their industry and patience, cheerful endurance of privation, and unswerving, yet not austere piety, mingled salutary elements with the character of this new western world.

JOSEPH WARREN.

MAJOR GENERAL JOSEPH WARREN was born in Roxbury, in 1741. His father was a respectable farmer in that place, who had held several municipal offices to the acceptance of his fellow-citizens. Joseph, with several of his brothers, was instructed in the elementary branches of knowledge at the public grammar school of the town, which was distinguished for its successive instructors of superior attainments. In 1755 he entered college, where he sustained the character of a youth of talents, fine manners, and of a generous, independent deportment, united to great personal courage and perseverance.

On the 18th of April, 1775, by his agents in Boston, he discovered the design of the British commander to seize or destroy our few stores at Concord. He instantly despatched several confidential messengers to Lexington. The late venerable patriot, Paul Revere, was one of them. This gentleman has given a very interesting account of the difficulties he encountered in the discharge of this duty. The alarm was given, and the militia, burning with resentment, were, at daybreak on the 19th, on the road to repel insult and aggression. The drama was opened about sunrise, within a few yards of the house of God, in Lexington. Warren hastened to the field of action, in the full ardor of his soul, and shared the dangers of the day. While pressing on the enemy, a musket ball took off a lock of his hair close to his ear. The lock was rolled and pinned after the fashion of that day, and considerable force must have been necessary to have cut it away. The people were delighted with his cool, collected bravery, and already considered him as a leader, whose gallantry they were to admire and in whose talents they were to confide.

On the 14th of June, 1775, the Provincial Congress of Massachusetts made him a Major General of their forces. He was at this time president of the Provincial Congress, having been elected the preceding year a member from the town of Boston.

Several respectable historians have fallen into some errors in describing the battle in which he fell, by giving the command of the troops on that day to Warren, when he was only a volunteer in the fight. He did not arrive on the battle-ground until the enemy had commenced their movements for the attack. As soon as he made his appearance on the field, the veteran commander of the day, Colonel Prescott, desired to act under his directions; but Warren declined taking any other part than that of a volunteer, and added, that he came to learn the art of war from an experienced soldier, whose orders he should be happy to obey. In the battle, he was armed with a musket, and stood in the ranks, now and then changing his place, to encourage his fellow-soldiers by words and example. When the battle was decided, and our people fled, Warren was one of the last who left the breastwork, and was slain within a few yards of it, as he was slowly retiring. His death brought a sickness to the heart of the community, and the people

mourned his fall; not with the convulsive agony of a be-
trothed virgin over the bleeding corpse of her lover, but with
the pride of the Spartan mother, who, in the intensity of her
grief, smiled to see that the wounds whence life had flown
were on the breast of her son, and was satisfied that he had
died in defence of his country.

This eminence has become sacred ground. It contains in
its bosom the ashes of the brave who died fighting to defend
their altars and their homes.

Within a year after his death, Congress passed the following
resolution : —

"That a monument be erected to the memory of General
Warren, in the town of Boston, with the following inscription : — *

IN HONOR OF

JOSEPH WARREN,

MAJOR GENERAL OF MASSACHUSETTS BAY.

HE DEVOTED HIS LIFE TO THE LIBERTIES OF HIS COUNTRY,

AND IN BRAVELY DEFENDING THEM, FELL AN

EARLY VICTIM IN THE

BATTLE OF BUNKER HILL,

JUNE 17, 1775.

The Congress of the United States, as an acknowledgment of his
services and distinguished merit, have erected this
monument to his memory."

The preceding memoir is taken from the Monthly Magazine,
published in Boston, June, 1826, and is the production of Samuel L. Knapp, Esq.

The following monument stood near the site of the present
Bunker Hill monument: —

---

* To the lasting honor of the Congress of '76, the above resolution
was passed, but, after the lapse of three quarters of a century, we
ask, Where is the monument? A petition is now in preparation, to
present to the next Congress, praying them to carry out the patriotic
resolve of their predecessor.

Erected A. D. 1794, by King Solomon's Lodge of Free Masons,
constituted at Charlestown, 1783,

IN MEMORY OF

MAJOR GENERAL WARREN
AND HIS ASSOCIATES,
who were slain on this memorable spot, June 17, 1775.

"None but they who set a just value upon the blessings of liberty
are worthy to enjoy her
In vain we toiled, in vain we fought, we bled in vain, if you, our
offspring, want valor to repel the assaults of her invaders!"

Charlestown Settled, 1628; Burnt, 1775; Rebuilt, 1776.
The enclosed land given by Hon. James Russell.

John Warren.

THE personal appearance of Dr. Warren was most prepossessing. He was of about middling stature, and well formed; his deportment was agreeable, and his manners, formed in a military school, and polished by intercourse with the officers of the French army, were those of an accomplished gentleman. An elevated forehead, black eyes, aquiline nose, and hair turned up from the forehead, gave an air of reflection and dignity, which became a person of his profession and character. His remains are deposited in a tomb erected for the purpose by his family, in the cemetery of St. Paul's Church, in Boston. In the same sepulchre rest the relics of his friend and brother. — *Thacher's Medical Biography.*

H. J.

J O H A N N E S   W A R R E N,

Bostoniensis,

Temporibus suis illustris,

Nec posteritati obliviscendus.

Bello civili semper rei publicæ deditus,

Juventutem patriæ sacravit.

Medicus inter primos,

Chirurgus facile princeps,

Novangliæ

Primam medicinæ scholam,

Ipsius laboribus fundatam,

Per xxx. annos

Doctrina sustulit,

Eloquentia illuminavit.

Quid verum, quid honestum,

Quid scientiæ, quid bono publico profuturum

Exemplo docuit,

Vitæ studio promovit.

Erga Deum pietate,
Erga homines benevolentia sincere imbutus,
Summam severitatem
Summæ humanitati junxit.

Universitatis Harvardianæ Professor,
Societatis Philanthropicæ Præses,
Societatis Medicæ Massachusettensis Præses,
Nullus illi defuit honos.
Vita peracta non deest omnium luctus.

Natus die xxvii. Julii, A. D. MDCCLIII.
Obiit die iv. Aprilis, A. D. MDCCCXV.

—

In this Tomb
Are deposited the earthly remains of
MAJOR GENERAL JOSEPH WARREN,
Who was killed
in the Battle of Bunker Hill,
on the
17th June, 1775.

———

Timothy Bigelow. (Worcester.)

In memory of
TIMOTHY BIGELOW, ESQ.,
Commander of the 15th Massachusetts Regt.
In the Revolutionary war with Great Britain.

Born August 12, 1739.
He died April 4, 1790,
Aged 50 years.

Here lie his Remains.

The above-mentioned Timothy Bigelow was an officer of

great merit and distinction in the Revolution. He commanded a battalion of Arnold's forces in the chivalrous expedition through the wilds of Maine to Canada, and was taken prisoner in the attack upon Quebec, on the night when Montgomery was slain. After being exchanged, he was again in active and responsible service for several years. The regiment which he commanded was raised mainly by his own exertions, in the central parts of the state. He left five children, viz.: Anna, Timothy, Lucy, Rufus, and Clara. Anna married Dr. Abraham Lincoln, of Worcester, (brother of the first Governor Lincoln,) who was afterwards a member of the executive council. Lucy became the wife of Luther Lawrence, of Groton, a lawyer, who subsequently was a prominent member of the legislature, and mayor of Lowell. Rufus became a merchant, and settled in Baltimore, where he died, unmarried, in 1814. Clara married her cousin, Tyler Bigelow, of Watertown, a lawyer, and left several children, among whom are Clarissa, the wife of Theodore Chase, a merchant and ship owner of Boston; Charles H. Bigelow, now of Lawrence, late a captain in the army; and George Tyler Bigelow, a justice of the supreme judicial court. Timothy, the eldest son of Col. Timothy Bigelow, was born April 30, 1767, graduated at Harvard in 1786, was admitted to the bar in 1789, and became a distinguished jurist and legislator. He was speaker of the house of representatives for eleven years; died at Medford, May 18, 1821, aged fifty-four. He married Lucy, daughter of Judge Oliver Prescott, of Groton, (brother of William Prescott, of Bunker Hill memory.) She still survives, in a green and honored old age. Her eldest daughter, Katharine, born 1793, is the wife of Abbott Lawrence, minister of the U. S. to Great Britain. The sons are, the Rev. Dr. Andrew Bigelow, born 1795, and John Prescott Bigelow, born 1797, now mayor of Boston.

John Brooks.

Sacred to the Memory of
J O H N   B R O O K S ,
who was born in Medford, in the month of May, 1752,
and educated at the town school.
He took up arms for his country on the 19th of April, 1775.
He commanded the regiment
which first entered the enemy's lines at Saratoga,
and served with honor to the close of the war.
He was appointed Marshal of the District of Massachusetts
by President Washington;
and after filling several important civil offices,
he was, in the year 1816, chosen
Governor of the Commonwealth,
and discharged the duties of that station for
seven successive years, to general acceptance.
He was a kind and skilful physician;
a brave and prudent officer;
a wise, firm, and impartial magistrate;
a true patriot, a good citizen, and a faithful friend.
In his manners he was a gentleman;
in morals, pure; and in profession and practice,
a consistent Christian.
He departed this life in peace, on the 1st of March, 1825.
aged 73.
This monument to his honored memory
was erected by several of his fellow-citizens and friends,
in the year
1 8 2 5 .

BELOW is an engraving of a monument about to be erected in Roxbury, in memory of John Eliot, the Apostle to the Indians.

John Eliot

JOHN ELIOT,
THE APOSTLE TO THE INDIANS,
Died at Roxbury, May 20th, 1690,
In the 86th year of his age.

Index.

A.

	PAGE
Adams, Abigail	- - 56
Adams, Alexander	- 7
Adams, Daniel -	- - 180
Adams, Elijah	- - 130
Adams, Elizabeth	- - 68
Adams, Isaac	- - 69
Adams, James -	- - 35
Adams, John	- 10, 132
Adams, John -	- - 137
Adams, Jonathan	- 78
Adams, Mary	- 73, 112
Adams, Nathaniel	- - 4
Adams, Samuel	- - 180
Adams, Thomas -	- 116
Adlington, John	- - 109
Adlington, Rebecca	- 109
Allcock, Abigail	- - 160
Allen, Andrew J. -	- 192
Allin, Edward -	- - 45
Archer, Ann	- - 92
Armstrong, Mary	- - 104
Atkins, Silas	- - 49
Attwood, Elizabeth -	- 31
Attwood, John	- - 31
Attwood, Joshua	- - 31
Attwood, Mary	- - 22
Augustus, Mary	- - 107
Austill, Elizabeth -	- - 16
Austin, Joseph	- - 181
Aves, Isaac -	- - 110

	PAGE
Aves, Samuel -	- - 145
Ayre, Emeline A. -	- 40
Ayre, J. Cullen	- - 40
Ayres, Abigail	- - 5
Ayres, Antoinette D.	- 40
Ayres, John	- - 134
Ayres, Nathanie	- - 15

B.

Babcock, Samuel	- - 99
Badcock, Samuel	- 159
Badger, Albert -	- - 146
Badger, Esther	- - 146
Badger, Frances Maria	- 146
Badger, Martha Emma	146
Badger, Stephen	- - 146
Badger, William -	146, 182
Baker	- - - 183
Baker, Alexander -	- 122
Baker, Elizabeth	- - 123
Baker, Josiah	- 85, 123
Baker, Mary	- - 122
Bailey, Adams	- - 165
Ballard, Dorcas	- - 18
Ballard, Elizabeth	- 171
Ballard, Sarah	- - 85
Balls, Martha	- - 144
Balls, Robert -	- - 144
Bankamp, John -	- 51
Barber, John -	- 101, 149

Barber, Nathaniel - -	141	Boardman, Aaron - 144
Barber, Robert - -	- 181	Boies, Margaret - - 52
Barker, Polly Tidmarsh	166	Bommor, Margret - 127
Barnard, Alce - - -	76	Bommor, Thomas - - 127
Barnard, Elizabeth -	50, 87	Bound, James - - 133
Barnard, John - -	- 66	Boutcher, Mary - - 160
Barnard, Mathew - -	76	Bowles, Joshua - 11, 206
Barnard, Thomas -	- 33	Bowles, Mary - - - 11
Barr, Susanna - -	61	Boyden, Simeon - - 158
Barrons, Leonard -	- 26	Boynton, William - - 88
Barry, Thomas -	- 126	Bradburn, Richard - 177
Barstow, Jacob -	- 177	Breading, Abigail - - 119
Barter, James -	- 27, 69	Breading, Phillip - - 77
Bartlett, James -	- 156	Breck, S - - - - 35
Bass, Moses - - -	75	Breed, Sarah - - 85
Bass, Phillip -	- - 91	Brewer, Nathaniel - - 150
Bass, Sarah - - -	80	Brigham, Hannah - 121
Bassett - - -	- 175	Brigham, Peter - - 194
Bassett, Mary -	- 145	Briggs, John - - 50
Battens, John - -	- 86	Brondson, Elizabeth - - 33
Baxter, Rufus -	- 166	Broun, Lydia - - 6
Beal, Abigail - -	- 32	Brown, Ann - 151, 183, 184
Beal, Caleb - -	74	Brown, Charity - - 94
Beale, Abigail - -	- 95	Brown, Elizabeth - 51, 119
Beath, Joseph	88, 110, 117	Brown, Hannah - - 66
Beath, Seeth - -	- 110	Brown, John - - 93, 184
Beatly, Ralph -	- 62	Brown, Jonathan - - 169
Beer, William - -	- 34	Brown, Josiah - - - 172
Beers, Ann - -	- 193	Brown, Martha - - 86
Belcher, Elizabeth -	- 38	Brown, Mary - - - 183
Bell, Edward -	- 156	Brown, Nathaniel - 117, 182
Bell, Shubael - -	- 198	Brown, Nicholas - - 51
Bennet, Ellis -	- 59	Brown, Samuel - - 94
Bennet, Mary -	- 122	Brown, Sarah - - 53, 208
Bennit, Sarah -	58, 195	Brown, Thomas - - 119
Bently, Susan - -	- 85	Brown, William - 92, 183
Berry, Elizabeth -	- 43	Buckley, John - - 62
Berry, Grace - -	- 4	Buckley, John, Jun., - 66
Bigelow, Timothy -	- 235	Buckley, Joanna - - 26
Bill, Abigail -	- 64	Buckley, Joseph - 17, 26
Binney, Amos -	- 164	Bull, Joseph - - 31
Binney, Benjamin -	- 164	Bull, Mary - - - 7
Binney, Joshua -	- 164	Burbeck, William - - 101
Blackador, Mary -	- 52	Burbeck, Jerusha - - 101
Blackman, Rebeca -	94	Burchisted, Ann - 190
Blake, Deborah -	- 127	Burdsell, Jane - - - 74
Blake, Joseph -	- 149	Burdett, James W. - 90
Blanchard, Marcy -	- 165	Burke, Mary - - - 138

Brooks, John	- - - 237	Clark	- - - 170
Burke, William	- - 138	Clark, Hannah	- - 21
Burril, Jane	- - - 179	Clark, Jonas	- - - 30
Burrill, Ann -	- - 178	Clark, Joseph	- - 21
Burrill, Mary	- - - 179	Clark, Josiah	- - - 11
Burrington, Elizabeth	- 74	Clark, Margaret	- - 21
Burrough, William	- - 22	Clark, Prudence	- - 21
Burt, Abigail	- - 55	Clark, Sarah 21, 22, 30, 105
Burt, Benjamin	- - 55	Clark, William -	- - 102
Burt, John	- - - 55	Clark, William F. -	- 158
Burt, Samuel	- - - 55	Clarke, Johannis	- - 103
Burt, Susannah	- - 55	Clarke, Rebecca	- - 17
Burt, William	- - - 55	Clarke, Robert -	- - 147
Butler, Sarah	- 57, 157	Clough, Ann	- - 32
		Clough, John -	- 27
		Clough, William -	- 52
C.		Cocke, Joseph -	- - 187
		Cole, Isaac -	- - 121
Cabot, George -	- - 192	Cole, Rachel C.	- - 121
Cabot, Martha	- - 192	Coleman, Elizabeth	- 44
Caddall, Jerusha	- - 77	Coleman, Temperance	- 44
Cades, Abigail	- - 84	Colesworthey, Judet	- 153
Cadwell, John -	- - 185	Collacott, Richard	- 9
Callender, Joseph -	- 151	Collins, Charity -	- 79
Calley, Joseph -	- - 105	Collins, Clement	- - 77
Campbell, Alexander	- 47	Collins, Hannah -	- 96
Capen, John	- - - 157	Collins, Patience	- - 79
Capen, Patience	- - 24	Collins, Sarah	- - 96
Capen, Thomas	- - 167	Coney, Mary -	- - 15
Capron, Christopher -	150	Connel, Patrick	- - 42
Carnes, Edward	- - 11	Cook, Cornelius	- - 159
Carnes, Thomas -	- 199	Cook, Ellis -	- - 150
Car. Rebecca -	- - 150	Cookson, John -	- - 148
Carter, Jane -	- - 100	Cooper, Abigail -	- 18
Carter, John	- - - 100	Cooper, John Lambord	- 113
Carthew, Hannah -	- 69	Coping, Ann	- - 158
Cary, Jonathan	- - 169	Copp, Amy -	- - 30
Chamberlin, Jane -	- 72	Copp, David	- - - 14
Champney, Caleb Dinsdal	194	Copp, Hannah -	- - 30
Champney, Sarah	- 191	Copp, Joanna	- - 1
Chapin, Elizabeth	- - 5	Corlew, Elijah -	- - 68
Chew, Prince	- - 133	Crawford, David -	- 52
Christy, Hannah	- - 112	Crease, John -	- - 123
Christy, John	- - 113	Creighton, Mary -	- 67
Christy, Thomas	- 20, 112	Crocker, Abigail	- - 55
Claflin, Warner	- - 193	Crowlley, Joseph -	- 180
Clap, Henry	- - - 168	Crozer, John -	- - 166
Clapp, Caleb	- - 132	Cullam, Lydia	- - 63

Cumby, Rebecca - - 78
Cumby, Robert - - 78
Cumings, Bradle - - 184
Cushing, Benjamin - 183
Cushing, Daniel - - 224
Cushing, John - - 224
Cutler, Elizabeth - - 198
Cutler, Timothy - - 198

D.

Dalton, Michael - - 158
Darling, Betsey - - 80
Darracott, George - - 150
Davis, Isaac Howard - 157
Davis, James - - 185
Davis, O. and S. - - 193
Delaplace, Thomas - - 15
Demount, Dorcas - - 73
Dennen, James - - 185
Dennis, Michael - - 112
Dethick, John - - 84
Dickenson, Daniel - 196
Dissmore, Fanny - - 172
Dixwell, Martha - -37
Dixwell, Mary - - 37
Doak, Nathaniel - - 145
Dobel, Abigail - - 56
Dobel, John - - 56
Dobel, Joseph - - 57
Dobel, Mary - - 57
Dodd, William - - 72
Dodge, James - - 177
Dodge, Nabby - - 172
Dodge, Sarah - - 171
Domack, Nancy - - 62
Doncan, John - - 118
Dorrington, John - - 64
Doubelde, Dorcas - 35
Doubleday, Benjamin - 138
Doubleday, Susannah - 99
Dowrick, William - - 16
Draper, Moses - - 69
Drowne, Leonard - - 69
Dunblide, Sally - - 99
Duncan, Isabella - - 188
Duncan, Robert - - 188

Dunn, Susan - - - 148
Dupee, Isaac - - 60

E.

Eames, Samuel - - 194
Edes - - - - 49
Edes, Edward - - - 27
Edmonds, Hannah - 92
Edmunds, Robert - - 84
Edwards, David - - 85, 95
Eeles, Thomas - - - 172
Ela, Mary - - - 90
Eliot, Andrew - - - 124
Eliot, John - - - 215
Elliot - - - - 190
Elliot, Maria - - 33
Ellis, Joshua - - - 40
Ellis, Joshua, Jun. - 40
Ellis, Lydia L. - - - 40
Ellis, Sarah - - - 40, 75
Ellis, William - - - 59
Emerson, Henry D. - 40
Emerson, Parker, Jun. - 193
Emmes, Martha - - 36
Euerden, Abigail - - 151
Eustis, Benjamin - - 42
Eustis, George - - 94

F.

Farmer, Mary - - - 141
Farnum, Charles - - 8
Farnum, Joseph - - 83
Farmer, Paul - - 20
Farrington - - - 196
Faxon, Nathaniel - - 194
Felton, Luther - - - 191
Fennilly, Robert - - 198
Fenno, John - - - 173
Fernald, Elizabeth - 168
Feveryear, Joanna - - 179
Fifield, Eliza - - 23
Fisher, Jabez - - - 152
Fisher, Nathaniel - - 152
Fisk, Sewall - - - 115

Fisk, Thomas L.	- -	120
Fitzgerald, Mary	- -	147
Fletcher, Margaret	-	180
Fletcher, Nathaniel	- -	146
Forbs, Jonathan	- -	168
Forist, Mary	- - -	42
Forsyth, Elizabeth	-	106
Foster, John	- - -	121
Foster, Susannah	- -	174
Fracker, Thomas	-	91
Francis, William	- -	45
Frothingham, Eben	- -	195
Frothingham, Thomas	-	185
Fuller, Eliza	- - -	65
Furbur, Abigail	- -	16
Furbur, Richard	- -	68
Furbur, Richard, Jun.	-	68

G.

Gale, John	- - -	176
Gamman, Grace	- -	74
Gardner, Deborah	- -	112
Gardner, Mary	-	79, 115
Garish, Lydia	- - -	59
Gatte, Thomas	- -	93
Gay, Eben	- - -	184
Gay, Timothy	- -	108
Gee	- - - - -	140
Gendall, Lydia	- -	94
George, Daniel	- - - -	89
Gere, Eleanor	- -	43
Gilburt, Mary	- - -	10
Giles, Hannah	- -	64
Gill, Elizabeth	- - -	83
Gill, John	- - -	83
Gill, Nathaniel	- - -	25
Gill, Obadiah	- -	9
Gill, Obodiah	- - -	10
Gill, Samuel	-	9, 84
Gillander, Joseph	- -	48
Gilman, Abigail	- -	71
Gilman, Bethia	- - -	70
Gilman, Lydia	- -	71
Gilman, Peter	- - -	53
Gilman, Peter, Jun.	-	71
Glasier, Nathaniel	- -	148

Glidden, Joseph	- -	17
Goddard, Earl	- - -	191
Godmer, James	- -	90
Godner, William	- -	91
Goffe, Abigail	- -	46
Goffe, John	- - -	91
Goffe, Samuel	- -	28
Gooding, Richard	- -	116
Gooding, William	-	109
Goodrich, Henry	- -	188
Goodwell, Thomas	-	46
Goodwill, Thomas	- -	153
Goodwin, Benjamin	-	58
Goodwin, Hannah	- -	58
Goodwin, John	- -	18
Goodwin, Mary	- -	18
Goodwin, Nancy Heatherston	58
Goodwin, Sally	- -	70
Goold, Sarah	- -	103
Gordung, Abraham	- -	89
Gould, Charlotte	- -	164
Gould, Thomas	- -	169
Graham, John A.	- -	134
Grant, Ann	- - -	107
Grant, Edward	- -	6, 29
Grant, Elizabeth	- -	107
Grant, John	- - -	107
Grant, Mary	- - -	107
Grant, Moses	- -	107
Grant, Samuel	- - -	107
Grant, Sarah	-	84, 107
Grant, Susan W.	- -	107
Graves, Daniel	- -	83
Green, Eliza L.	- - -	168
Green, Hannah	- -	15
Green, John	-	16, 144
Green, Nancy	- -	167
Green, Thomas	- -	160
Greenogh, J.	- -	188
Greenough, Elizabeth	-	21
Greenough, William	-	105
Greenough, Dorythy	-	185
Greenough, Sarah	-	98
Greenwood, F. W. P.	-	217
Greenwood, Isaac	-	217
Greenwood, Mary	- -	32
Greenwood, Nancy	-	32
Greenwood, Nathaniel	-	14

Greenwood, Samuel - 24
Greenwood, Samuel, Jun. - 24
Greenwood, William Pitt 217
Griffin, Isaac - - - 6
Gronard, Joseph, Jun. - 47
Grover, Dean - - - 19
Grubb, Martha - - 106
Guliker, John - - - 143
Guliker, Mary - - 143
Guliker, Thomas - - 143
Gunderson, John - - 124
Gyles, Charles - - - 158
Gyles, Mary - - - 77
Gyles, Samuel - - - 118

H.

Hall, Jacob - - - 10
Hall, J. and M. - - 175
Hall, William - - 182
Hammatt, Benj. - - 50
Hammatt, Joseph - - 191
Hammatt, Marcy - - 173
Hammond, Elizabeth - 174
Hammond, Nathaniel - 193
Hancock, Ebenezer - 32
Hanyford, Abigail - - 131
Hares, Hezekiah - - 3
Hares, John - - - 3
Harper, Henretta - - 35
Harrington, Andrew - 194
Harrington, Mary B. - 146
Harris, Elizabeth - - 111
Harris, Hannah - - 98
Harris, John - - - 98
Harris, Nathaniel - - 99
Harris, Richard - - 19
Harris, Samuel - - - 29
Hartt, Edmund - - 63
Hartt, Lois - - - 13
Hartt, Mary - - 13, 203
Hartt, William - - - 191
Harvey, John - - 145
Harvey, Mary - - - 135
Hasey, Martha - - 7
Havvatt, Peter - - - 168
Haward, Abraham - - 141

Haward, Thomas - - 141
Hawkes, Ezra - - 169
Hawkins, Jacob - - 11
Hay, Theodocia - - 45
Hayden, Caleb - - - 155
Haywood, Anthony - 76
Heath, Deborah - - 181
Heath, Mary - - 147
Heath, Nathaniel - - 147
Heath, Samuel - - 181
Henchman, Anna - - 107
Henchman, Richard - 50
Henderson, B. - - - 172
Henderson, Hemmen - 61
Hemmenway, Susanna - 139
Hemmingway, Joseph - 65
Herman, Elizabeth - - 163
Herman, Eliza - - 163
Hewens, Jacob - - - 57
Hewins, Jacob - - 57
Hichborn, Samuel, Jun. - 167
Hicks, Mary - - 23
Hill, Charles - - - 146
Hill, Charles Stephen - 146
Hillard, Martha - - 138
Hill, Mary - - 63, 100
Hill, Nathaniel H. - - 146
Hill, Samuel - - 146
Hiller, George - - - 163
Hilman, Peleg L. - - 95
Hirsst, Hendrieth - - 87
Hoar, Willmouth - - 90
Hobby, Ann - - - 84
Hobby, Hannah - - 89
Hobby, John - - - 80
Holden, Nancy - - 62
Holland, John - - - 143
Holland, Samuel - - 192
Holland, Susanna - - 143
Holmes, Charles - - 114
Holmes, Francis - - 183
Holmes, Mary - - 46
Homer, Mary Ann - - 178
Hood, Joseph - - 21
Hooper, Rebekah - - 7
Hopkins, Caleb, Jun. - 170
Hopkins, Enoch - 62, 96
Hopkins, Samuel - - 65

Hopkins, Thomas - - 148
Hoskins, Katherin - 175
Hoson, John - - 117
Hough, Lydia - 8
Hough, William - - 22
Howard, Ales - - 6
Howard, Charles - - 147
Howard, Joseph - - 175
Howe, John - - 173, 176
Howe, William - - 176
Howland, Nathaniel - - 55
Hubbard, Elizabeth - 172
Hudson, Elizabeth - - 151
Hudson, Frances - - 13
Hudson, Thomas - - 193
Hughes, Mary - 89, 195
Hughes, Phillip - - 36
Humphres, Mary - - 45
Hunt, Ammey - - - 88
Hunt, Joab - - - 106
Hunt, Joanna - - - 156
Hunt, Judith - - 97
Hunt, Mary - - - 48
Hunt, Sarah - - 88, 106
Hunt, Thomas - - 57, 152
Hunting, Mary - - 9
Huntley, Mary - - - 104
Hurst, Hindreth - - 95

I.

Ibone, Godfrey M. - - 199
Ingersoll, Daniel - - 149
Ingersull, George - - 46
Ingles, James - - 61
Ingham, Abigail - - 20
Ingraham, Joseph - 144
Ireland, Grace - - - 151
Ireland, John - - 63
Irvalt, Henrietta - - 134

J.

Jackson, Ward - - - 174
James, Abigail - - 132
James, Francis - - - 130

James, John - - - 137
Jarvis, Charles - - - 38
Jarvis, Leonard - - 40
Jarvis, Elizabeth - - 41
Jarvis, Mary - - - 111
Jeffs, Anna - - - 115
Jeffs, Mary - - - 111
Jenkins, Isaac - - - 191
Jenkins, Solon - - 191
Johnson, Daniel - - 114
Johnson, Hans Peter - 130
Jones, Joseph - - - 161
Jones, Josiah - - 41
Jones, Mary - - - 41
Jones, Mercy - - 103
Jones, Richard - - - 25
Jones, Samuel - - 63
Jonson, Thomas - - 41
Josselyn, Emeline C. D. 40

K.

Kellon, Thomas - - 42
Kemble, Elizabeth - 120
Kemble, Thomas - - 76
Kenney, Elizabeth 25, 143
Kent, John - - - 79
Kent, Jonathan - - 115
Lent, William - - - 8
Kimble - - - 190
King, Elizabeth - - 67
King, Gedney - - 167
King, Josiah - - - 101
King, Robert - 43, 163
King, William - - - 100
King, William, Jun. - 100
Kingsbury, Jesse - - 188
Kinsman, Pelatiah - 77
Knight, Samuel - - 92
Knox, Martha - - 43

L.

Lack, Richard - - - 91
Lad, Briget - - - 189
Lake, Ann Worthy - - 13

21 *

Lake, George Worthy - 13
Lake, John - - - 3
Lake, Ruth Worthy - 13
Lake, Thomas - - 2, 201
Lambert, Thomas - - 149
Lamson, Elizabeth - - 46
Lane, Ammi - - 118
Lane, Elizabeth - 118, 167
Lane, Henry - - - 114
Langdon, John - - - 179
Langdon, Josiah - - 142
Langford, Hannah - - 25
Larrabee, Benjamin - 71
Lasenby, Marcy - - 111
Lash, Elizabeth - - 113
Lash, Johanna - - - 116
Lasinby, Thomas - - 53
Lawlor, Thomas - - 109
Lee, Deborah - - 34
Lee, Thomas - - - 34
Lemmer, Mary - - 127
Lewis, John - - - 160
Lewis, Mary - - - 70
Lewis, Nathaniel - - 121
Lewis, T. and J. - - 175
Libby, J. G. L. - - - 195
Lidston, Elizabeth - 46
Lincoln, Heman - - 174
Lincoln, Noah - - 166
Little, Alexander - - 136
Littlefield, Rebecca - 31
Long, Eliza - - - 135
Lord, Harriot - - 126
Lord, Polly - - - 126
Lord, Samuel - 124, 126
Lord, Thomas - - - 126
Loring, Benjamin - 222
Loring, Elizabeth - - 56
Loring, John - - 222
Loring, Jonathan, Jun. - 159
Loring, Josiah - 222
Loring, Joshua - - - 157
Loring, Thomas - 221
Low, Abiah P. - - - 170
Low, Abigail - - 47
Low, George - - - 170
Low, John E. - - 88
Lowd, William - - - 76

Lucas, Roger - - 136
Lucas, Sarah - - - 136
Luscomb, Thomas - 4

M.

Macomber, Ichabod - - 147
Malcom, Ann - - 44
Malcom, Daniel - - 12
Malcom, Sarah - - 78
Marden, David - - 159
Mariners' Tomb - 128, 215
Marshall, Francis - - 93
Marshall, Josiah - - 161
Marshall, Marcy - - 31
Martyn - - - 125
Martyn, Michael - - 20
Masse, Francis - - 176
Masters, Jonathan - - 68
Mather, Cotton - - 1
Mather, Increase - - 1
Mather, Samuel - - 1
Maverick, John - - 50
Mavericke, John - - 9
Mavericke, Mehitabel - 10
McClennen, William - 161
McKean, Elizabeth - - 67
McMillian, Ann - - 108
McMillian, Edward - - 108
McRedding, Edward - 199
Mellens, William - - 175
Merchant, Martha - 120
Merchant, William - 39, 120
Merells, Jeremiah - - 134
Merrills, Jeremiah - - 19
Merritt, Mary - - 69
Merritt, Phillip - - - 69
Michell, Rebecca - - 114
Mickell, Thomas - - 192
Miles, Experience - - 7
Milk, Eleanor - - - 178
Milk, John - - 34, 178
Milk, James - - - 178
Milk, Susannah - - 178
Mills, Eliza - - 87, 166
Mills, William - - 165
Miller, Anna - - - 114

Miller, Sarah - - 73
Millet, Abraham - - 164
Moore, Mary - - 184
Morrison, John - - - 62
Mortimer, Hannah - 82
Mortimer, James - - 82
Mortimer, Peter - 80, 135
Mountfort, Benjamin 3, 81
Mountfort, John - 3, 81, 203
Mountfort, Jonathan 81, 210
Mower, Samuel - - 117
Mulvana, Sarah - - 70
Mumford, William - 20

N.

Nelson, John - - - 156
Newel, Nathaniel - - 94
Newell, Nathanael, Jun. - 35
Newell, Prudence - - 98
Newhall, Hannah - - 122
Newhall, Henry - - 122
Newman, Robert - - 39
Newman, Robert, Jun. - 39
Newton, John F. - - 157
Nichels, Samuel - - 188
Nicholl, John - - - 122
Nichols, Hannah 33, 67, 90
Nickerson, Elijah - - 148
Norton, David - 97
Norton, Sarah - - - 179
Nottage, Nathaniel - 159
Nowel, Mary - - - 63
Nowel, Michael - - 19
Noyse, Samuel - - - 165

O.

Odin, John - - - 199
Oliver, T. - - - 169
Onesimus, Jane - - 42
Onesimus, William - 42
Otheman, Anthony - - 199
Otheman, A., Jun. - 199

Otheman, Hannah - - 199
Otheman, Henry - - 199
Otheman, Mary - - 199
Owen, Mary - - - 92

P.

Page, Edward 82, 99, 125, 164
Page, Mary - - - 123
Palmer, Grace - - 190
Parker, John - - - 98
Parker, N. - - - 174
Parker, Nathaniel - - 185
Parker, Sarah - - 98
Parkman, Alexander - 36
Parkman, Dorothy - 38
Parkman, Elias - - 27
Parkman, Elizabeth - 27
Parkman, Esther - - 36
Parkman, Hannah - 97
Parkman, Mary - - 120
Parkman, Samuel - 37, 207
Parkman, Sarah - - 120
Parkman, William - 38
Parkman, William Bowes 38
Parry, Cornelius Cook - 47
Parry, Lucy - - 47, 159
Parsons, Ebenezer - 82
Parsons, Edmund - - 146
Parsons, Edmund, Jun. 146
Parsons, James Winchell - 146
Parsons, Lydia - - 176
Patridge, Robert - - 75
Paul, Mary - - - 117
Paul, Moses - - - 117
Paull, Moses - - 93
Payson, Mary - - - 88
Payson, Moses Paul - 117
Pearson, Martha (Goodwin) 18
Peggy, Dorcas - - 68
Peirse, Elizabeth - - 23
Penwell, Ann - - - 150
Perkins, Mary - 61, 104
Perkins, Rebecca - - 127
Phillips, Dorcas - 67, 85
Phillips, James - - 133

Phillipes, John - - - 3	Reade, Annah - - 8
Phillipes, Johana - - 5	Redding, George - - 194
Pickerin, Elizabeth - - 6	Reed - - - - 183
Pierce, Hannah - - 190	Revere, Eliza Maria - - 124
Pierce, Mary - - - 190	Rhoades, Jacob - - 181
Piercival, J. - - - 174	Rhodes, Samuel - - 187
Pitman, Betsey - - 49	Richards, Abigail - 114
Pitman, John H. - - 111	Richards, John - - - 110
Pitman, William - - 142	Richards, Mary - - 29
Pittoni, John - - 9	Richards, Edward - - 110
Pittom, Mary - - - 24	Richards, Joseph - - 110
Pittom, Mathew - - 69	Richardson, Anne - - 124
Polley, John - - - 191	Richardson, Catharine - 124
Polley, William - - 193	Richardson, Isabell - - 124
Pomroy, Lucy - - - 48	Richardson, Phebe - 145
Pool, Ann - - - 75	Richardson, Thomas - 182
Pool, Anna - - - 131	Ridgway, L. - - - 49
Pool, Benjamin - 75, 131	Rind, Mary - - - 67
Poole, Mary - - - 176	Rind, William - - 67
Porter, Thomas - - 28	Ripley, Robert - - - 187
Potts, Thomas - - - 198	Ritchey, Sarah - - 138
Powell, Michael - - 6	Robbins, Thomas - - 49
Pratt - - - - 190	Roberts, Eliza - - 119
Pratt, Eleazer - - 220	Roberts, John - - - 119
Pratt, Joseph - - - 160	Roberts, John White - 71
Pratt, Meheteble - - 86	Roberts, Mercy - - - 72
Pray, John H. - - - 195	Roberts, Richard - - 152
Prentiss, S. - - - 173	Robertson, David - - 101
Prichard, John - - - 159	Robins, Polly - - 169
Proctor, Edward - - 144	Robinson, Elizabeth - - 13
Proctor. Eliza Lane - - 71	Robinson, George - 4
Pullen, John - - 158	Robinson, Simon W. - 184
Pullen, Mary - - 43, 158	Rose, Phillip - - 123
Pulling, John - - 30	Ross, Andrew - - - 171
Pullington, James - - 26	Ross, John - - - 171
Pulsifer, David - - 127	Ross, Margaret - - - 171
Pulsifer, Elizabeth - - 127	Ross, William - - 171
	Rous, Sarah - - - 65
	Rouse, William - - 29
R.	Ruby, Elizabeth - - 134
	Ruby, Ann - - - 79
Randall, Richard - - 92	Ruddock, John - - - 154
Randols, Michael - - 148	Rule, Sarah - - - 6
Ransford - - - - 196	Rumney, Edward - - 116
Ransford, Edward - 24	Rumney, Seeth - - 109
Rawlins, Love - - - 37	Russell, John - - - 22
Rayner - - - 183	Russell, Mary - - 93
Read, Eleanor - - - 43	R. Y. - - - - 96

S.

Salisbury, John	- - 4
Salsbury, Nichlas	- 4
Salter, Abie	- - - 125
Samuel	- - - 80
Sargeant, Elizabeth	- - 73
Sargent, Edward	- - 190
Sargent John	- - - 190
Sargent, Thadeus	- - 22
Sartly, Martha	- - - 39
Sarvise, Sarah	- - 61
Sawin, Ezekiel	- - - 147
Saxton, John	- - 5
Saxton, Nathaniel	- - 7
Scammell, Alexander	- 182
Scammell, Mary	- - 182
Scarlet, Elizabeth	- - 122
Scarlet, Mehetebel	- - 17
Schollay, John	- - 173
Scoot, Anna	- - - 126
Scoot, Thomas	- - 126
Scott, Mary	- - - 25
Seares, Robert	- - 20, 64
Sears, Alexander	- - 29
Sears, Hannah	- - 29
Senier, Joseph Shaw	- 10
Seward	- - - 106
Seward, Benjamin	- - 116
Seward, Catharine	- 106
Seward, James	- - - 106
Seward, Sarah	- - 12
Seward, Thomas	- - 12
Shapley, Henry	- - 130
Sharrow, George	- - 61
Sharp, Margary	- - 120
Sharp, Sarah	- - - 39
Shaw, Francis	- - 54
Shaw, Francis, Jun.	- - 54
Shaw, John	- - 55
Shaw, Nathaniel	- - 55
Shaw, Robert G.	- - 54
Shaw, Samuel	- - 54, 55
Shaw, Sarah	- - 10
Shaw, Sarah Burt	- - 54
Shaw, William	- - 55
Sheffe, Elizabeth	- - 30

Sherburn, Abigail	- 86
Sherburne, W.	- - - 171
Sherman, James	- - 178
Sherrin, Richard	- 96, 104
Sherrin, Sarah	- - 96
Shirley, James	- - 45, 137
Shute, Caleb B.	- - 186
Shute, Ebenezer	- - 186
Shute, Elizabeth	- - 5
Shute, Frances	- - 186
Shute, Joseph B.	- - 186
Shute, Susan	- - - 186
Shute, Susannan	- - 186
Shutt, Hannah	- - - 16
Shutt, Mary	- - - 16
Shutt, Martha	- - - 101
Sigourney	- - - 137
Sigourney, Andrew	- - 145
Simmons, Cornelius B.	182
Singleton, Ann	- - - 99
Singleton, George	- - 100
Singleton, James Carter 50, 100
Skillin	- - - - 142
Skillin, Mary	- - - 113
Skillin, Ruth	- - 113
Skillin, Simeon	- - 113
Smallpiece, Furnell	- 76
Smith, Arthur	- - 30, 44
Smith, Benjamin Shurtleff	197
Smith, Elizabeth	- 161
Smith, Hiram	- 197
Smith, Hiram Shurtleff	- 197
Smith, James	- - 161
Smith, James B.	- - 156
Smith, John	- - - 143
Smith, Julia Ann	- - 197
Smith, Nathaniel	- - 199
Smith, Susannah	- - 156
Smith, William Sullivan	197
Snelling, Anna	- - - 139
Snelling, Benjamin	- 138
Snelling, Elizabeth	- - 91
Snelling, Enoch H.	- 195
Snelling, Jonathan	- - 133
Snelling, Joshua	- - 133
Snelling, Josiah	- - 179
Snelling, Joseph	- - 139
Snelling, Margaret	- - 35

Snelling, Pedigree of - 238
Snelling, Priscilla - - 65
Snelling, Rebecca - - 66
Snelling, Sarah - 133, 165
Soames, Hannah - - 120
Soames, John - - - 95
Somes, Susannah - - 170
Spaulding, Leonard - - 176
Spear, Ebenezer - - 226
Spear, George - - 225, 226
Spear, Nathaniel - - 226
Spear, Richard - - - 226
Spear, Samuel - - 225
Spring, Samuel - - 177
Starling, John - - 189
Starling, Patience - - 189
Steel, William N. - - 114
Stephens, Eliza - - 166
Stephens, Elizabeth - 125
Sterling, Grace - - - 135
Stetson, Sarah - - 186
Stetson, Susan - - - 186
Stetson, Susan G. - - 186
Stevens, Erasmus - 43, 163
Stevens, Mary - - 28
Stevens, Patience S. - - 126
Stevens, Sarah - - 28
Stevens, Thomas - - 28
Stockwell, Asahael - 157
Stoddard, Abigail - - 23
Stoddard, Elizabeth - 24
Stoddard, Hannah - - 11
Stoddard, Mercy - - 153
Stoddard, Thomas - - 23
Stone, Anna - - - 152
Stone, Elizabeth - - 105
Stow, Emily - - - 129
Stone, Josiah - - - 150
Stone, Nicholas - - 57
Stone, Sarah - - - 152
Stookas, Sarah - - 137
Stretton, Elizabeth - 73
Sullivan, Charles G. - 108
Sumers, Mary - - - 90
Sunderland, John - - 53
Suter, John - - - 196
Sutherland, George - 79
Sullivan, James G. - - 107

Sullivan, John - - 149
Sullivan, Thomas - - 149
Swaen, Sarah - - 37
Sweet, John - - - 89
Sweat, Susanna - - 89
Sweetser, Benjamin - - 195
Swier, Lucy - - - 95
Swift, Edee - - - 59
Swift, Elijah - - - 58

T.

Taylor, Abigail - - 78
Templer, Thomas - 52
Thacher, Mary - - - 13
Thatcher, Margaret - 77
Thaxter, Jonathan - - 166
Thayer, Alonzo - - 130
Thayers, Cotton - - 91
Thayer, John - - 156
Thomas, Abigail - - 20
Thomas, Ann - - 149
Thomas, Ann R. - - 149
Thomas, Elizabeth K. - 136
Thomas, Harvey - - 15
Thomas, Mary - 97, 149
Thomas, Peter - - - 136
Thomas, Samuel - - 149
Thompson, Robert - - 189
Thornton, Thomas 162, 217
Thornton, Sarah - 56, 210
Thornton, Timothy 56, 209
Tilden, Robert L. - - 41
Tileston, John - - 101
Tilton, Hannah - - 121
Tompkins, George - 83
Tompkins, Isaac S. - - 172
Tomson, Benjamin - 132
Tomson, Susannah - - 167
Tout, Elizabeth - - 59
Tout, Mary - - - 59
Tout, Sarah - - - 59
Townsend, Ebenezer - 131
Townsend, James - - 37
Townsend, James R. - 131
Townsend, John - - 131
Townsend, Judith - 74, 131

Townsend, Polly	-	72, 131
Townsend, Sarah	-	- 118
Travis, Daniel	-	- 90
Trefry, William	-	- 173
Treuis, Jean -	-	- 58
Trew, Richard -	-	- 91
Trout, William	-	- 23
Tucker, Daniel -	-	- 95
Tucker, Martha	-	- 61
Tufton, Elizabeth	-	- 116
Turell, Elizabeth -	-	109
Turner, Jonathan	-	- 186
Tuttle, Hannah	-	- 52
Tuttle, Turell -	-	- 160
Twing, Rebeca	-	- 75
Tyer, William -	-	- 7
Tyler, Dorcas	-	- 123
Tyley, Elizabeth	-	- 36

U.

Upshall, Nicholas	-	- 219
Urann, Joseph	-	- 156
Utley,	-	- 183

V.

Vannevar, Alexander	-	177
Vannevar, George	-	187
Varney, James -	-	- 142
Varney, Jean	-	- 142
Veazie, Eli	-	- 184
Vernon, Fortesque	-	48
Vernon, Thomas C.	-	- 48
Vial, Elizabeth	-	- 44
Vpshall, Dorathy	-	- 8
Vpshall, Nicholas	187, 219

W

Wade, John	-	- 189
Wadsworth, Susannah	-	19
Wakefield, Eliza	-	- 188
Wakefield, Samuel	-	87
Wair, Lydia	-	- 44

Waldo, Ann -	-	64
Wales, Sarah -	-	- 15
Walker, Francis	-	- 196
Walter, Lynde -	-	- 199
Walter, William	-	- 199
Ward, Fransis -	-	- 8
Ward, William	-	- 180
Wardell, George	-	- 161
Warfield, Rebecca	-	19
Waterhouse, John	-	- 26
Waters, Mary	-	- 78
Waters, William	-	- 72
Watson, James	-	- 17
Watson, Mary -	-	- 17
Watts, Lydia	-	- 59
Watts, Richard	-	- 155
Way, Kathron	-	- 73
Weare, Elizabeth	-	- 5
Webb, Daved	-	- 36
Webb, Margaret	-	- 152
Webb, Thomas	-	- 153
Webber, Elizabeth	-	- 139
Webster, Grant	-	- 33
Weeks, Samuel	-	- 200
Wells, Charles	-	- 189
Wells, John	-	- 189
Wells, Nathaniel	-	- 189
Wells, Samuel -	-	- 82
Wheelen, Joseph -	-	183
Wheelwright, Elizabeth	-	200
Wheelwright, Joseph	-	199
Whellen, Richard	-	- 132
White, Hannah	-	- 25, 28
White, John	33, 105, 181
White, Katherine -	-	181
White, Marcy -	-	- 41
White, Mary	-	- 131
White, Sarah -	-	- 33
White, Susanna	-	- 170
Whitehead, Samuel	-	94, 194
Whitman, Davis -	-	165
Whittemore, Gershom	-	26
Whittemore, Lydia	-	86
Wild, Ebenezer	-	- 140
Willard, Josiah	-	- 44
Williams, Elizabeth -	-	87
Williams, John	-	- 34
Williston, Ann -	-	- 47

Williston, Joanna - - 118
Williston, John - - 47
Willson, Marcy - - 149
Winchester, Amasa - - 189
Winchester, Edmund - 177
Windsor, Ann - - - 75
Windsor, Hannah - - 131
Winslow, Mary - - 8
Winslow, Samuel - 97, 192
Winslow, Sarah - - 86
Wise, Daniel - - 157
Wiswall, Elizabeth - - 93
Wiswall, Peleg - - 111
Woodbury, Hannah - - 18
Wooddard, Prissiella - 121

Worthylake, Ann - - 151
Worthylake, George - 151
Worthylake, Ruth - - 151
Wotton, Elizabeth - 134
Wyer, John - - - 177
Wyman, Hezekiah - 53

Y.

Yendaell, S. - - - 193
Young, Hannah - - 176
Young, Joseph - - - 174
Young, Rachel - 164, 187
Young, Rebecca - - 180

TORREY MONUMENT AT MT. AUBURN.

www.ingramcontent.com/pod-product-compliance
Lightning Source LLC
Chambersburg PA
CBHW070610270326
41926CB00013B/2495